# I Know Who I Am When I Belly Dance!

**Also by Daleela Morad, M.A.**

Belly Dance Wisdom for Fitness, Pregnancy and a Divine Sexuality

# I Know Who I Am When I Belly Dance!

*A Handbook for Reclaiming Your True Feminine Self*

**Daleela Morad, M.A.**

## Dedication

This book is dedicated to my sisters on the belly dance path. May you fully embrace the power and beauty of the Divine Feminine and help uplift humanity and our Great Mother, the Earth.

# Acknowledgments

I would like to thank the following people whose support and suggestions have guided me in writing this book.

First, I would like to thank my husband, Joaquin Martinez, for being an amazing anchor both in my writing and in my life. Also, I wish to thank my daughter, Andrea Echegaray-Martinez, for carrying on the tradition of the belly dance.

I truly appreciate the encouragement from my friend and mentor, Majida Magdalena, my dance partner, Crystal Berger, my student and friend, Donna Emmerich, and my friend, Nadia Elias, all belly dance sisters along the path, who encouraged my dance performances or took the time to read chapters from my book with enthusiasm and support.

I am really grateful for all the time and effort Curtis Grant took to design another wonderful book cover. I am also grateful to Tommy Gleason for the amazing cover photo, and to Larry Grant for contributing the photography inside the book. I am thankful to Vincent Wales for his editorial assistance with the beginning of the book, and to Matthew Perry for his suggestions on the back cover.

I am inspired and awed by the contagious enthusiasm and dedication to this art by my students and troupe members from *The Eye of the Cobra*: Sarah Arizaga, Sarah Chessher, Donna Emmerich, Ching-I Chen, Tyronda Miller, Marilyn Designer, Theresa Radke and Camille Roxburgh.

For her refreshing enthusiasm, encouragement and professional insights, I am most grateful to my editor, Cathy Dean.

# Table of Contents

You can take away the Nile, you can take away the pyramids, but you cannot take away the belly dance.
*Egyptian Proverb*

"I'll have faith in God only if he dances."
*Nietzsche*

"It is the mission of all art to express the highest and most beautiful ideals of man. To express what is the most moral, healthful and beautiful in art - this is the mission of the dancer, and to this I dedicate my life."
*Isadora Duncan, The Art of the Dance*

# About the Author

Daleela Morad earned her Master's Degree in Counseling Psychology before practicing as a mental health professional. She also holds an Adult Teaching Credential in the Performing Arts, and a minor degree in music from the University of California, Davis. She fuses her 19 years of expertise in Middle Eastern dance with 10 years of experience as a counselor to offer belly dance therapy for women. As a University of California Regents Scholar, author, artistic director, performer, choreographer, and dance instructor, she wishes to spread the healing power and beauty of the feminine through the ancient art of belly dance.

Daleela has been performing for over 19 years and is known for her passionate, joyful, and mesmerizing dances. Led by her passion for Middle Eastern dance, Daleela travels and performs internationally and leads workshops on belly dance and on the therapeutic aspects of belly dance. Daleela studied with numerous Egyptian dance masters and has performed in mystical Egypt, as well as in Latin America and Asia. She has written travel stories and articles about the therapeutic aspects of belly dance for acclaimed dance magazines El *RaksEL Sharki, Zaghareet*, and *The Gilded Serpent.*

*The Sacramento Metropolitan Arts Commission has* certified Daleela to teach and perform three educational workshop/performances to K-12 schools and community organizations. In 1998, she won the prestigious *Elly* award for her lead role as the gypsy dancer, *Esmeralda*, with Garbeau's Family Theatre in Sacramento, California and also starred as *Scheherazade* and *Pocahontas.* She appeared on the December, 1997 cover of the Middle Eastern dance magazine of oriental dance and arts, *"El Raks El Sharki."* As the featured dancer, she choreographed and danced in the East Indian documentary film, *Daulat*. She lives with her husband, Joaquin Martinez, and teenage daughter, Andrea, in Sacramento, California. She and her daughter carry on the tradition of the belly dance, performing together as a

mother/daughter duet for many celebrations. She and her troupe, *The Eye of the Cobra*, dance for Northern California events to celebrate the power of women joined together. Visit www.daleela.com to find out more about Daleela's performances, classes, and workshops, to read about her dance travel stories to Egypt, Costa Rica, Nepal, and India, or to purchase her instructional DVDs and her performance DVD, *Healing Dances for the Human Heart.*

Dancers from left to right: Tyronda, Ching-I, Daleela, Theresa, Sarah

*Eye of the Cobra* photos by Joaquin Martinez

# Daleela Morad

# Introduction

## A Transforming Healing Art

In my first book, I introduced the belly dance with step-by-step, how-to dance instructions, as well as shared the meaning of the dance, its connection to childbirth, its history and my own dance story. In this book, I hope to lead you to deeper, transformative aspects of the dance and its capacity to heal your body, mind and soul. After 19 years of dancing, I am inspired to present a book that offers belly dance as more than a sensual art. I am inspired to offer the belly dance as the purest form of art: *a transforming healing art.*

Belly dance has the power to enable us to integrate the feminine and masculine within us so we may achieve balance in our lives. Many of the moves no doubt came from our ancestors observing different aspects of nature: a leaf quivering in the wind, ocean waves and a snake's undulations. Belly dance therefore offers a means for us to harmonize with Mother Nature. Being quintessentially feminine, belly dance teaches us to connect to attributes we call feminine. I believe that as we come to value these attributes we define as feminine (compassion, understanding, cooperation, creativity, intuition, and the ability to set boundaries and to care for ourselves as well) we usher in the traits humanity needs at this dire time in history.

As a belly dancer, I experience the strange sensation that I live in three completely different worlds. Throughout the day, I find myself preoccupied with my dutiful roles as wife, mother and wage earner. Then, in my classes, I transport myself into a beautiful, time-honored, ancient past where the pace of life is slow, soft, sensual and oriented toward nature.

Finally, while performing, I become a glamorous, sexy and sophisticated woman of the world. Whew…no wonder I'm tired by the end of the week!

Like many men and women, I grew up learning to devalue feminine attributes as inferior to male attributes. But, as I continued with my dance studies, I found myself slowly becoming a different woman. Dancing with bare feet connected me to nature and to the Earth, moving to the powerful rhythms of the drum grounded me, dancing soft, circular movements connected me to a healthy sensuality and a primal female energy I had lost long ago.

As I learned to belly dance, I began to recognize the strength and power inherent in female qualities. I began to connect to a long lineage of women who identified with their feminine natures, who were in tune with the cycles of the moon and connected to their bodies in a way modern women are not.

A belly dancer is often the shadow side of the modern day woman who lives from her neck up, too busy to feel, too stressed to enjoy her body, always doing, but rarely *being*. A belly dancer is an earthy woman, connected to her feelings, to gravity, to the soles of her feet. She is a creature of the earth, often symbolic of motherhood, possessing rounded hips and a belly. She is a powerful earth woman who is aware of the spirituality inherent in her sensuality, and who honors her body and her feelings. She is not about denying her flesh or her emotions, but about embracing both body and feelings in honor of the Divine Earth Mother.

To belly dance means to slow down, to connect to one's body and deep feelings, to go back before the advent of modern civilization when our ancestors lived closely connected to nature and to one another. This dance art epitomizes female energy at a primal level. It embodies all traits thought of as earthy and therefore female. As we learn to value all that is feminine, including nature and the belly dance, we will learn to value our Mother, the Earth.

Our planet needs tremendous healing. I think both men and women feel this need on some level. What can we do? As men and women, we can begin to value the feminine within ourselves in order to value our Mother, the Earth, the feminine without. But we cannot do this if both sexes continue to deny the value of female attributes, if we continue to live detached from our feelings, our bodies and our feminine spirits. We must all embrace and heal our feminine sides in order to heal the planet.

**Belly Dance as Therapy**

Because this is where my experience and knowledge lie, I will write primarily from the female perspective *addressing* women. However, there are many men who belly dance, and who gain similar benefits from this ancient art form. Throughout this book, please keep in mind that much of what I share about this dance may also apply to men who study the art.

The exercises, meditations, suggestions and advice given in this book are not intended as a *substitute* for a good therapist, but may be used as a supplement to professional counseling.

Belly dance affords you the opportunity to begin to heal from deep inner pain, to start to discover your lost sensuality and the power of feminine energy (within both sexes). You will learn how with the appropriate focus, belly dance may serve as a tool to begin healing yourself at an emotional, mental and spiritual level.

You probably realize that belly dance is a great strength training and aerobic workout, but you may not know that it also possesses the power to alleviate depression, help heal sexual trauma and connect to others through mutual empowerment and healing.

When I encourage you to belly dance, I recommend this as a professional therapist and as a professional dancer. As a dance teacher, I have seen many shy and introverted women blossom into confident and powerful dancers. This confidence and sense of personal power often translates into their day-to-day lives. I have seen women who were ashamed of or disconnected from their femininity embrace their female traits and female power. I have witnessed young girls who started dancing as young as age five learn to love their developing bodies. They gained a sense of themselves as women as they developed into adulthood.

Connecting to your body through music and movement may help you release repressed feelings. Unlike your thoughts and feelings, your body eventually reflects whatever difficulties you may be encountering. Your body will never lie to you. If you are chronically depressed, your posture, stance and gait will quickly reveal this. If you have carried anger for a long time, your muscles will become chronically tense. If you have not yet released a past trauma, your body will hold onto the emotional impact of the trauma and often manifest the emotions as a physical illness or as pain.

From the onset of this book, I want to make crystal clear that when I suggest belly dance as a therapeutic path, I don't suggest you aim to dance professionally. On the contrary, it is more therapeutic to dance for fun, at home with a video, an inspiring book, or in a class with a good teacher who will introduce you to the joys of the belly dance.

**Belly Dancing to Mend a Broken Heart**

Have you ever felt addicted to a man? After he left you, did you feel as though you would never feel alive again or ever fall in love again? This chapter shares how belly dancing may become addictive also, but in a good, life-giving way, not like an unhealthy, life-draining relationship. In this chapter, I share a short story about how Sylvia was able to break her addiction to a man who wasn't good for her and how she found a deep feminine power and wisdom again. At the end of the chapter, you will find a list of what to do to begin to mend your broken heart.

**Belly Dancing to Alleviate Depression**

Belly dancing allows you to begin to heal the emotional wounds lodged in your body, wounds often created by societal beliefs that result in devaluing the feminine. Through belly dancing, you will learn that traits thought of as female, such as creativity, receptivity, sensitivity, sensuality and empathy, are powerful, *not weak,* once you own them and use them to balance your masculine traits.

Also, belly dance may act as a powerful moving meditation with the capacity to alleviate depression simply by releasing your pent-up anxieties, fears, and anger, feelings we all experience throughout our lives at some time or another. Using belly dance as an avenue for emotional expression and for experiencing a greater connection to one's body is immensely therapeutic for depression. Because depression is characterized by feelings of hopelessness and helplessness, once you begin to experience greater mastery over your body and emotions, these feelings may lift. The basic body stance in belly dance, which thoroughly grounds you, by itself begins to create a foundation of physical strength and begins to free up old patterns of disassociation and repression.

You will discover the power to begin to lift yourself out of depression by embracing a dance companion that will never leave you. As a belly dancer, you have an outlet for unacknowledged feelings or fears. As you begin to own your repressed side (or shadow side), you will learn to value your power as a woman and rediscover your self-esteem.

**Reclaiming a Healthy Sexuality**

Belly dance may help heal your sexual wounds. Can you think of a better way to push your sexual hang up buttons than through connecting to the sexuality of your body as you gyrate your hips, undulate your belly and shimmy your shoulders? Learning this ancient dance becomes a beautiful opportunity to face your fears and begin to heal. Connecting to your sensuality is the first step to connecting to your life energy and to creating healthy sexual patterns.

If you have suffered from physical or sexual trauma, at a very basic, instinctual level, you may claim ownership over a body you may have dissociated from long ago. You may recapture the sensual joys you once experienced prior to having been traumatized. You may connect to and then release the trauma lodged in your body by owning your pain. You may come to integrate all the scattered aspects of yourself into a unified whole.

**A Mental Discipline**

Mentally, this dance is a focused discipline, requiring your dedication and practice, as well as your creativity. Because the dance demands that you learn to isolate numerous muscles, it requires tremendous concentration, focus, determination, practice and patience. It is as much a mental discipline as it is a physical discipline. As with any dance form, learning dance steps, combinations and traveling steps will help you to improve your memory and spatial abilities. Also, pouring your mental energy into dancing will make your daily troubles seem miles away. You will leave your workout or class feeling energized and ready to take on the world. This dance is a marvelous mental stress reducer.

**Enlivening Your Marriage**

Because belly dance helps you become fit as well as helps you learn to accept your body as it is, you will actually become more beautiful and more sensual for your significant other, as well as for yourself. As you become stronger, both physically and emotionally, this will transfer over into your love life. You will learn fifty delightful ways to entice your lover using role-plays, Arabian fantasies, belly dance sexual techniques, tantric sex principles and the element of surprise. You will use your aphrodisiac powers to entice your husband or to find a husband!

After many years of being with the *same* person, you may add spice to your marriage or significant relationship. If you feel your marriage is stale or down in the dumps that sense of playfulness, joy and romance that initially drew you to your beloved will return. Your husband or lover may himself heal as a result of your own healing. You and your marriage may come alive like never before!

**Connecting to Your Spirituality**

So what is spiritual about belly dance? Belly dance possesses the capacity to connect you to the feminine face of God because it is earthy and feminine. As a woman who belly dances, you will have the opportunity to tap into qualities often devalued by the larger patriarchal social system, qualities such as sensuality, sensitivity, intuition, receptivity and emotional expression. You will begin to feel more alive through valuing feminine aspects of yourself you may have previously denied, minimized or devalued.

As a spiritual discipline, the dance will never let you down. On the contrary, with the appropriate focus, belly dance may become a spiritual path or even your "church" as one of my fellow dance teachers put it. It may become a means for you to connect to the Divine Feminine or to Mother God. Because it epitomizes the feminine, it connects you to a primal female energy you may have disassociated from years ago in order to become successful in a man's world. In the following pages, I invite you to reclaim this primal female power, because it is your birthright.

# Belly Dancing to Mend a Broken Heart

For many of us, there is no greater pain than losing a loved one through a break-up, divorce or death. There is no greater ache than the grief, anger, and feelings of hopelessness associated with the loss of a love. Break-ups are an inevitable part of our lives, and so it is to our benefit to learn how to cope with the pain.

When Sylvia began to realize that her boyfriend, Stephen, simply didn't have the time (or rather wouldn't make the time) for her, that his career appeared to be more important to him than she was, she felt her tears flow like an unleashed dam. She splashed an ice cold glass of water on her face and told herself, "I need to leave him, cold turkey." But, when he gazed at her longingly with his captivating blue eyes, and lightly brushed his hand against her long legs, she could not bring herself to ignore his sweet apologetic voice and the incredible aphrodisiacal power of his kiss on the nape of her neck.

Every time she went to his apartment with the sincere intention to break it off, she ended up melting into his muscular arms instead. Stephen, who used to be a boxer, would then pick her up, run his fingers through her long blond hair, lightly brush her rosy cheeks, and she would find herself falling into his bed again.

She continued to see him only when he had the time. Despite the fact that most of the time he was too "busy" to return her calls right away or return her emails (sometimes she had to wait over a week) she convinced herself she was just being a "big baby." She convinced herself that she had no claim on him and to stop being so "needy." After all, they weren't married or engaged.

9

He convinced her that he had a right to his life the way he wanted it, and she simply needed to honor what he was *able* to give her at this time in his life. "You just need to love me as I am. After all honey, I love you just as you are, with your big hips and all."

She couldn't give herself the permission to tell him *she* also needed to be honored for what *she* wanted in the relationship. Somehow, it seemed Stephen's needs were more important because he was still struggling to develop his business selling fine jewelry. She already had a great career as a journalist with a magazine company that hired her years earlier, the day after she received her B.A. She remembers how proud her family was and how they celebrated by taking her out to her favorite place for dinner.

In the back of Sylvia's mind, she pondered the possibility that maybe he had *another* girlfriend. Her fantasies ran away with her. Did he give her beautiful golden pearl earrings as well? Did he take her for romantic day hikes and skinny dip with her under the moonlight at Ice House Lake, her favorite spot in the entire world? Did he make her his homemade, delicious crepes for breakfast? Most people she knew just didn't work until 11 PM night after night completing paperwork from the office.

But, she dismissed the idea as fantasy. "I have got to stop being so damn insecure," she told herself. She trusted him when he stated, "Of course there isn't anyone else; most of my free time goes to you. Just because I don't call you back right away does not mean you aren't important to me. Of all the people in my life, I see you the most. I wouldn't have time for another girl even if I wanted one." This made logical sense to her. "Besides," he added, "I could never find another woman with eyes as emerald green as yours." And that last statement usually did the trick.

In her moments alone, despite his sweet words, she was tired of feeling unimportant and abandoned. Why couldn't she just make a clean break from him? Why couldn't she leave him once and for all? Why was she so weak; what kind of hold did this tall, blond and handsome man have over her? Night after night she went to bed searching, seeking, asking for a dream, *any* dream, a daydream even, where she would find some answers. Was she addicted to this relationship? How could she be? She was a strong, intelligent, professional woman with a great job, a nice house, and an active social life.

Sylvia shared with me that she walked in a daze during that time, baffled because she couldn't figure herself out. She would come home from work, walk through her front door, plop herself on the leather couch, and then just sit there and cry. She had always prided herself on being gifted in understanding others. So why couldn't she understand what was going on with herself? "I just think too much," she chided herself.

One day after work as she was browsing the internet, waiting for Stephen to return her call, she came across a belly dance website. The site stated: *Dance your sorrows away through the elegant and healing art of belly dance.* She later shared with me: "To say I was intrigued is an understatement. I had always thought of belly dancing as fun and great exercise, but never as boyfriend therapy!"

Driven by a force she couldn't explain, she immediately enrolled in my Sunday night class. The moment Sylvia entered the room, she told me later, she immediately felt she had come home. She began to rediscover herself. As she learned the movements, she embraced an earthy power that she had previously repressed. She began to connect to a lineage of women who, long before modern civilization, she learned from her research, were the original healers and teachers of humanity. Sylvia realized there was a power inherent in the belly dance that western dance forms did not possess. Because the dance required that she move her pelvis, abdomen, and hips, it helped her connect to areas of her body western society had taught her were sexual and therefore shameful. She began to own parts of her body western culture taught should be rail thin to look beautiful. She had always disliked her hips; they were too big. She had never been happy with her abdomen; it was too rounded. But the dance helped her *embrace* her full hips and belly as sacred and reflective of her innate power as a woman. The dance helped her view her pelvis as the seat of life and therefore sacred. She began to reclaim a feminine wisdom she had been oblivious to all her life.

Sylvia went home that first night, refreshed, revived, and excited about her new hobby. Wow, not only was this hobby fun, but it possessed something deeper than she could put into words. She emailed her best friend, Denise, and told her all about the class. She and Denise had danced in many ballet recitals together as children. But belly dancing was so different from ballet. It allowed for a fuller figure, didn't require that she dance on pointe, and she greatly enjoyed moving her hips and pelvis. She went home and practiced daily for a good hour, that first week, and the week after that, and the week after that.

For three weeks, she immersed herself in the mesmerizing and exotic world of belly dance. She browsed the internet at work during her free time (whoops, her boss caught her twice), at home before bed, and on weekends. She bought three belly dance books and began to read them, all at the same time. She wrote to other belly dancers that she met on www.buzz.com, the largest online belly dance community. She discovered there existed a whole other world she had not fathomed in her wildest imagination, and it was all about the wonderful world of belly dance.

At the start of the third week of belly dance class, she received a text message from Stephen that he had time to meet with her next week before his big out of country trip. She read the message:

*I'm sorry honey I haven't had time to call you all week. I just get home so late and so exhausted every night that I crash on the sofa and forget to call you.*

She asked herself out loud, "What kind of an apology is this?" If this text message was an apology, it sure didn't feel like one. He simply forgets about her because he is too tired? She's tired after work, too, but all she thinks of is Stephen.

Along with the text message, there was a voice mail from her belly dance instructor: "Would you like to dance at our student show coming up in a week? I know this is fairly last minute, but you are a very fast learner and I think the experience would be fun and rewarding."

This message excited Sylvia more than Stephen's message. *To hell with Stephen; I am going to dedicate my body and my sensuality to my dance. I don't need a man like him.* Ignoring his text message, she went out and bought a five hundred dollar, handmade in Egypt, gold-sequined bra and belt set, a one hundred dollar gold lame skirt, and a beautiful, fifty dollar rainbow colored silk veil.

"Six hundred and fifty dollars! That's a lot of money." her mother told her. "Are you sure it's worth it?"

"Maybe not the costume mom, but I am worth every penny."

Now she felt like a *real* dancer. In her new costume, every day for two hours, she practiced the five-minute routine she learned in class. She fell in love with the haunting, melodic music and the soft, serpentine movements. They carried her out of her head and into her body, heart, and soul, parts of herself she usually ignored as she went about her hectic day.

The night of her performance, Sylvia received many compliments from the other students in her class, from her family, and from her dear friend, Denise. Denise reminded her, "Since high school I have been telling you, you should pursue dance. You were the star of that last play you did your senior year because of your dancing, remember? Sylvia, your heart and your spirit shine when you dance. I am so glad you *finally* took my advice."

Her mother and sister told her she radiated as though she were in love. *Strange, they never told me that when they saw me with Stephen! On the contrary, they told me I looked worn out.*

Sylvia discovered she *was* in love, with her newfound talent, her stronger body, and the powerful sensuality she had unleashed in her life. Whoops! She didn't realize she hadn't called Stephen until he left a phone message the day after her show.

"You are probably mad at me, dear, since I am not hearing from you. I am sorry if you feel neglected, but I made it clear to you from the start that I am building a career right now, and so I am not ready for a commitment. I hope you are still OK with that. I hope you still don't think I am seeing another woman."

She thought to herself, *I am not mad at him at all. Hell, I don't even miss him. Damn, I don't even care if he has another girl; I forgot I even had a boyfriend. Well, that's a first! What's going on here? Could it be that I have embraced a new love?*

Sylvia called Stephen five days after receiving his phone message and told him, "I am sorry I didn't get back to you right away, sweetie. I have just been so busy with my dance classes and shows. Thanks for honoring where I am and for just appreciating what I am able to give you at this time in my life."

They broke up a week later because *he* felt ignored and disrespected.

As a dance instructor/therapist, I am not surprised at the number of women who tell me they find belly dancing helps them break away from relationships that aren't working for them. I believe it is because it helps them create a stronger relationship with themselves. Later on, the *right* man comes along. I am also amazed at the number of women who are able to revive stale, long-term relationships just a few short months after they begin a class.

As a woman connects to her pelvis, her hips, and her belly in an intimate manner, she awakens something deep and powerful within herself, something ancient, something beautiful, and something incredibly sensual, possibly for the first time in her life. Some of my East Indian friends believe the dance awakens the Kundalini energy. Kundalini energy is one's dormant spiritual energy, the serpentine-like energy coiled at the base of the spine that, once awakened, travels up the spine to the crown of the head enlivening one's soul and spirituality.[1] I imagine that long ago when this dance originated, our female ancestors intuitively understood the belly dance to be an avenue for awakening this dormant energy, for awakening a spiritual and sensual passion often missing in their lives. And maybe this feminine spirituality and sensuality is missing in our lives too?

If you are a woman who feels alone in your marriage, in a stale marriage (see the chapter on *How to Enliven Your Marriage*), misunderstood by your husband, or feel that your husband is *not spiritual enough,* this art form may help you connect to a sisterhood sorely lacking in western society today. You may find yourself dancing with like-minded women for personal healing and growth. You may reclaim your matrilineal line, your inner feminine wisdom, and your female power.

Your age, your shape, and your size do not matter. No one is asking you to perform professionally for others. You only need to dance for yourself.

Kimberly, a former student of mine who has had negative experiences with past lovers cheating on her, is very careful with the men she dates, and chooses to remain single. A former model, she could get any man she wants. A beautiful redhead with a strong, lithe, athletic body, she simply does not want a boyfriend. She does not feel ready to commit to *another* relationship. Until she decides she is ready, she states that belly dancing has done wonders for her self-esteem, for loving her body, and she feels sexy and sensual without having to be with a man. Kimberly states that belly dance has helped her learn to love her body in a way no man ever has, to value and cherish her body as sacred and profound, as a gift from the Great Goddess herself. She claims that, like a lover, this dance art soothes and comforts her, makes her feel sexy and beautiful, and gives her plenty of excitement. However, unlike most of her past lovers, it is reliable, and will never cheat on her or leave her.

She says, "It is the perfect mate for me at this time."

Although she has chosen to remain celibate for the last three years, she connects to her body and her sensuality in a completely safe and non-threatening way. I admire Kimberly because she has developed her talent to the point that she now performs regularly at weddings, anniversaries, birthdays, and other special occasion events, and this is a huge accomplishment for her. She feels appreciated and beautiful, sexy and young, all without having to be in a relationship. In fact, belly dance has proven to be better for her than a boyfriend because in most of her relationships, her partners' lack of fidelity *injured* her power, beauty, and sensuality.

When Kimberly is ready, I know she will take the chance again and choose to be in a relationship. But, this time it will be out of love for herself and her body, rather than out of a *need to be loved*. We must all strive to honor ourselves in this way.

## How to Begin Mending a Broken Heart by Belly Dancing

1. When you feel the urge to call, email, or text your ex, do one or more of the following:

   - Practice your moves or your routine from dance class.
   - Purchase an instructional DVD and practice, practice, practice. I have several available through my website: www.daleela.com, or check out the resource section in the back of this book.
   - Go to a music store and buy a belly dance CD.
   - Attend a workshop taught by a master teacher. Online, you will find dance masters such as *Alexandra King, Ansuya, Artemis, Atlantis, Dunia, Farida Fahmy, Judeen, Tito, Raquia Hassan, Suhaila Salimpour,* and many more

to see if they may be coming to your area. A good site is: www.dancemasterofbellydance.com.

- Browse belly dance sites (please see the resource section for some great sites).
- Go on www.youtube.com and you will find countless belly dancers from all over the world. This alone will distract you for hours and days without end.
- Start working on a costume. See my first book, *Belly Dance Wisdom*, for step-by-step instruction on how to make your own costume.

2. Have a belly dance party. Invite your fellow dance classmates, friends, and family. Dance for them and teach them some cool moves. Share any DVD's or costumes you may have and soon they'll be joining the class with you.

3. Go to student shows, even if just to observe. This will help you network with other like-minded dance souls and become less dependent on *him* for fun and support.

4. Read a good belly dance book. See the resource section in my first book. *Snake Hips,* by *Anne Soffee,* is a great book to read after a break-up. It is the story of how a woman found love through belly dance, after her first boyfriend dumped her. You can find it on Amazon.com.

5. Choreograph a dance in which you act out your grief or anger toward your lost love. Pick sad music that moves you and just allow your body to move in whatever way it needs to in order to

express your grief. See the next chapter, *Alleviating Old Wounds and Depression,* for dance exercises to help relieve grief.

# Alleviating Old Wounds and Depression

## Catholic School Girl

*High School Wallflower*

As the colorful disco lights shone upon my partner and I, we merged, two dancing rainbows transformed into a magical kaleidoscope of color and sound. Like a passionate lover, the steady disco beat entered my body, and I *became* one with the rhythm. My thoughts gone, and my heart filled with joy, I let the music dance me. Connecting to the music with my body, heart, and soul always transformed me. I was no longer a self-conscious teenager. As I let myself go, I felt truly alive and intimately connected to a force larger than my own life. As an adolescent, dancing became one of the few moments I felt connected to my core self. *I knew who I was when I danced!*

But, as I walked the halls of the snobby Catholic High School I half-heartedly attended, I became the epitome of the shy, lonely adolescent. I spent most of my first year lunch hour hiding in the bathroom and waiting in the snack line. hid the fact that I ate alone by eating my lunch in the bathroom stall. Returning to the lunchroom, I then entered the long snack line, bought a snack and simply returned to the back of the line, *over and over again*. This way no one caught me eating alone at a table. But, I needn't have worried. All those years, no one noticed anyway because I made myself invisible. All the more reason I relished those precious moments dancing under the rainbow lights. I lost myself in the rhythms and momentarily forgot the painful ache of my aloneness.

## *Model Child*

To cope with feelings of unimportance, I overcompensated by becoming an honor student. Since I can remember, I compulsively strived for straight A's! Furthermore, I rarely disobeyed my parents, never broke curfew, and I never, ever skipped school! On the contrary, I constantly strove to please my parents or other adults, even if it meant finking on my younger fourteen-year-old brother.

One day, I caught my younger brother taking my father's brand new Mercedes for a joyride around the block. Like a good, responsible first-born, I tattled on him. Needless to say, the grown ups liked me. However, being popular with the adults, meant my peers did not think I was so cool.

But, the cute, blond boy I danced with under the colorful disco lights thought I was cool! Nick exemplified the all-American kid: handsome, blond, a football player, popular, and *cool*. One night at a school dance, Nick completely surprised me, "Would you like to dance with me?"

My heart raced and I felt the palms of my hands sweat. I felt my eyes become huge as saucers before I could finally muster a simple, "OK." This guy was too cool for me. To add icing to my dance cake, Nick was also two grades higher than me.

"I love the way you dance," he exclaimed smiling at me with his soft, baby blue eyes.

*Wow, he must really be drunk or on pot, to ask ME to dance,* I thought.

We danced for five minutes, mesmerized, lost in the music, the lights, and in the movements of our bodies.

*This is too good to last,* I thought. Just then, as though reading my mind, a dark-haired beauty cut in and literally pulled Nick away from me. Tipsy, no doubt from drinking or smoking pot, Nick went along with her without struggle. Caught by surprise, I stopped dancing and sat down, too embarrassed to continue dancing alone.

Curious to know what had transpired, but trying not to appear conspicuous, I calmly looked over my right shoulder. Handsome Nick sat nonchalant between his sister, Tina, and her best friend, Natalie. Disgusted, Natalie eyed me with furrowed brows. She then whispered into Nick's ear. My stomach doubled up in knots; I knew she was saying something about *me* and I knew she wanted me to know she was doing just that!

Not wanting a confrontation, I quickly stood up and looked for another dance partner, but, to no avail. Two boys turned me down. They were not about to be seen dancing with a brainy "square".

Later that evening I saw Nick sitting by himself, staring down at his feet, and sighing once. Perhaps he missed me? But he didn't ask me to dance again that night. However, later that evening, I mustered up the courage to ask him about the incident. Half-drunk, he had little difficulty telling me what Natalie had whispered in his ear: "What are you doing with her? You could do so much better!"

## I Wasn't Good Enough

During my junior high and high school years, there were other incidents similar to this one. As a teenager living in Arizona, an outspoken boy named Nathan who loved to dance became the life of the parties I attended.

Once, halfway through a boring birthday party, he quickly stood up, proudly walked toward the edge of the outdoor patio where his friends sat, thrust his chest forward and outstretched his arms as he shouted, "I really like this song. Come on, doesn't anyone want to dance?"

He aimed his shouts toward the "cool" girls seated across the lawn. They simply giggled. At that same moment, hurrying to the little girl's room I inadvertently ran straight toward his open arms. Looking alarmed, he quickly pulled his arms in, turned away, and bolted in the opposite direction.

As I ran past him, I heard him exclaim to his many friends, "Thank God…I wanted to dance, but not *that* bad." They all laughed heartily.

Another time, I mustered up the courage to ask a basketball player, Michael, to the Christmas Formal. It was girl's choice. He immediately turned me down. He politely told me another girl had asked him first.

"Oh, I am sorry I didn't ask you first," I responded, "Who's the lucky girl?" He told me her name: Natalie. That's right, the same girl who whispered to Nick, "She's not good enough for you". To add insult to injury, the next day my friend Jennifer overheard Michael brag that I had asked him to the formal. She heard him say to his basketball buddies as he spat on the parking lot after school, "Yuck, I would never go out with her! I am hoping Natalie will ask me to the dance."

But somehow it was the incident with Nick that hit me the hardest. I knew Natalie was jealous because *she* liked him. I knew he was attracted to me and that was a big threat to her. But, I never confronted either of them. Probably because I convinced myself they were right. After all, I myself couldn't believe that Nick asked me to dance. *What possessed him? I am not cool enough for him. He must have been too drunk or stoned to notice that I was not of his caliber. Maybe his friends dared him to ask me.* These were the things I told myself.

Today, I realize this boy did like me. As a matter of fact, as I look back, that following Monday in between classes, in the school hall, he had smiled at me and said hello. Most important, he had said it while *sober*. Nonetheless, hurt because he never stood up for me, I turned my head away and completely ignored him. He said hello to me *all week*, but feeling hurt and indignant, I continued to walk the other way. The problem was not Nick; the problem was that I didn't like myself.

**Cultural Crisis**

As a young teen, I never thought of myself as voluptuous or sexy. On the contrary, I was a late bloomer with small breasts and small hips. First, I thought I was too skinny, and then I thought I was too fat. When I was thin, I yearned to be voluptuous with larger hips and breasts. So I ate more and finally gained weight only to discover I had gained twenty pounds more than I needed. Now I was chunky! Oh, the trials and tribulations of adolescence. Like most women, I have worked hard to maintain or lose weight ever since.

Today, young girls have an even more difficult time liking themselves and feeling whole. Delilah, a renowned belly dance teacher and performer, discusses this issue:

"Those of us raising adolescent girls in our society are aware of the cultural crisis affecting young women's personal growth and self-identity."[2]

Delilah reminds us that among American girls there is more depression, eating disorders, addictions, self-mutilations and suicides than ever before! She points out how the best-selling book, *Reviving Ophelia,* by

Mary Pipher, Ph.d, offers parents strategies to cope with this crisis. The book is based on the character of Ophelia from Shakespeare's "Hamlet," who is destroyed by her loss of self. However, I don't believe it is only young women who need to revive themselves. In a society that worships youth and beauty, middle-aged and older women also need revival.

## Real Values

Learning to love my body and femininity through belly dancing was one of the ways I counteracted the powerful media images depicting "perfect" female bodies. I learned to see beyond the superficial perfectionism of a youth and sex-obsessed culture. As a result, I came to embrace what Delilah calls "real values," which include "nourishing our creative spirits, practicing compassion, and taking care of our families, communities, and our Earth."[3]

I also developed my creative and intuitive abilities by creating my own choreographies. I developed my sensitivity as an artist and began expressing my emotions through dance. Through dancing with others, I experienced a sense of community, and I began to like myself and other women. As I began to fulfill my own needs, I became more compassionate and empathic toward others and toward my own family. I began to value the things in life that really mattered, including our Earth.

Delilah shares what she discovered in her twenty years of teaching women to belly dance: "I'm really teaching them how to reclaim lost parts of themselves. This is cause for celebration, hoot and holler! How did we get so lost? I have found that it is this opportunity of rediscovery that women all over the globe love about this dance form. They love the chance to open up, love, feel, and reacquaint themselves with their own hips, butts, belly, breasts, faces . . . the women that come to my classes seek a way to keep themselves from falling apart."[4]

## How We Become Depressed

Nadia Gamal, once premier belly dancer of the Arab world, emphasized the importance of emotional expressiveness in the *danse orientale*. Most of the well-known dancers I viewed while visiting Egypt are very expressive with their faces and eyes, as well as with their bodies. This is because an Arabic audience actually prefers a dancer who dances with heart and feeling to one who may be technically superior but cold or mechanical. They understand this dance is not simply about being sexy, but about expressing what it means to be fully human, capable of a broad range of human emotion. Because they are a part of life, the emotions of grief and suffering, as well as joy, must be acknowledged in the dance.

When you cut yourself off from your feelings, from your body, believe your worth is measured by your beauty, or feel a lack of connection to others, you are disconnecting from who you are at your core. Then you may no longer feel alive and understandably become depressed. Our culture teaches us to value our intellect and rational mind over our emotions, which are perceived as feminine and thus suspect or weak. The result is you may become very effective at shutting down your emotions and your five senses. You may not realize you have become a walking zombie.

The other modern day cause of depression, which is characterized by a feeling of helplessness and hopelessness, often stems from childhood beliefs developed from being a victim of physical, sexual or emotional abuse. These beliefs of helplessness may have served their purpose when you were a young child learning to get out of an abusive parent's way. But, they no longer serve you as an adult and may only lead to feelings of learned helplessness and hopelessness.

Another root cause of depression is western culture's unrealistic depictions of physical beauty. This cult of beauty conditions women to overly identify with their bodies. Many of us learn to like ourselves according to how attractive we *believe* you are, and most of us don't measure up to the unrealistic standards beauty magazines and other media hold. Imagine a world where every young girl grows up with a mother who belly dances? Imagine a world where all young girls take up belly dancing as part of their school curriculum. I have a suspicion the entire planet would change. Why? Because, there may be nothing more therapeutic, there may be no better role model for a developing young girl than to see her mother love and connect to her body in a healthy, sensual manner. Our society does not allow for this. Unfortunately, many of our images of the ideal woman are geared toward a perfection that does not exist. Today, most women yearn for this perfection, believing it will make them happy.

This unhappiness with our bodies is reflected in the beauty industry. It does not surprise me that plastic surgery is a multi-billion-dollar industry. In 2000, a survey conducted by the American Society of Plastic Surgeons (ASPS) concluded that two-thirds of patients have had more than one cosmetic procedure. The numbers are increasing at an alarming rate; ASAPS reported that, during 2003, 7 million women (16% increase from 2002) and 1.1 million men (31% increase) had plastic surgery.[5]

Finally, many of us feel alone and unsupported because we do not have a strong support system. We do not have the help from extended family members that our forefathers possessed when they lived in tribes, clans, and small villages. If you are a mother, married or not, you may often feel alone in raising your children due to increasing physical distances between family members that simply didn't exist in earlier times. Despite all these causes of depression, you can regain a sense of connection to your feelings, to your body, and to your fellow human beings.

**Feeling Alive Again**

How do you begin to feel the joy of living again? One of the best ways to combat depression is simply to *move*, to dance out your feelings. Don't sit in your depression. As you begin to move, you will start to connect to your body and to your feelings. You will feel stronger and in control. Also, you will begin to feel beautiful and graceful. Finally, feelings of loneliness will lift as you connect to other women and to the core of who you are: a powerful and joyful being meant to enjoy life. This latter belief will be more helpful in getting you through life than a belief in helplessness!

The mind and the body are connected, so bringing joy to one affects the other. Listen to your favorite uplifting music and allow it to carry you away. Or imagine that you truly are happy and bring that feeling of joy into your dance. Emotions create chemical reactions that foster physical sensations. So, as you recall the way your body looked and felt at moments of happiness and joy, you are actually creating the *same* emotion in your body. You are promoting positive chemical changes through your recall and visualization.

How do you allow your body to convey memories of joy? While remembering a joyful event from your past, feel this joy centered in your heart area, imagine this joyful feeling flowing outward through your arms, hands, legs, feet and face. Be true to yourself and allow yourself to embrace the joy you once felt as a child. Dance out the joyful and divine life force that propelled you into this life. I firmly believe none of us came here by accident. We were meant to come into this physical existence not necessarily to suffer but to joyfully express ourselves. So, allow yourself to feel alive again! Simply expressing the feeling of joy as you dance is therapeutic. You will begin to condition your body to know what joy *physically* feels like.

One of the most healing experiences I've had is dancing with very little clothing outside on a sunny day, preferably in a natural setting. Try a park, forest, mountain, ocean, or other nature setting with your favorite music. If you have a very private backyard, I recommend dancing completely **naked** under the sun. It is incredibly healing! The closest I have gotten to this is by belly dancing in my two-piece costume in the forest. It is difficult finding a place to dance naked without feeling vulnerable or getting arrested! I don't recommend this unless you know you are absolutely safe and unwatched. And, by all means bring a friend.

**Belly Dancing in the Rain Forest**

I encountered one of the most joyous experiences of my life dancing in my two-piece costume in the middle of the Tortuguero Rain Forest in Costa Rica. A group of native children between ages five and nine appeared out of nowhere to watch in fascination as I joyously danced between two jungle trees, sweeping two silk veils through the air in a myriad of swirling patterns.

Truly mesmerized by the soft flowing veils, the oldest child, Javier, ran home to tell his mother, "There is a woman *dancing* in the jungle." To make a long story short, that evening his mother invited me to perform for a group of travel agents from all over Latin America who were attending an annual conference. Javier and the other children came to watch. I shared the joy of the belly dance with this audience in a hot mosquito proof, screened in lodge in the middle of the Costa Rican jungle! I joked later to my friends back home that I had a nine-year old manager in Costa Rica. You can read the complete story on my web site www.daleela.com.

When depressed, we loose our natural sense of joy, feel alone and think we must endure life's turmoil's solo. In our postindustrial society, we have lost our connection to our Earth and to her seasons. We ignore the inner wisdom within us that says we are more than our bodies, more than our looks, more than our age, more than our weight. In our modern-day life, as women, we have been conditioned to overly identify with our bodies. We have lost our connection to our spirits and to our souls. Many of us fear we are losing ourselves most *as we age*. We fear no one will want us once we reach mid life or old age. We fear we may end up alone and unwanted by the opposite sex.

**Unlearning Our Education**

As a young woman, I often felt out of touch with myself and with my body. The Church told me my body was prone to sin and susceptible to evil. Many of the priests and nuns in the catholic schools I attended taught me I was born with original sin, and my emotions were not to be trusted. As a result, I feared that if I connected to my emotions or to my body, I would unleash repressed, sinful impulses and desires. What's more, through the concept of original sin, which states we are *born* with sin because Adam and Eve ate the apple, the Catholic Church taught me that as an infant I was already tainted with a black mark on my soul! What's more, the bible taught me that it was a woman named Eve who first ate the apple and tempted the first man, Adam, too fall. It was a bit difficult to like myself after hearing all of that!

It wasn't only religion that taught me to distrust and dislike myself. Rather than focus on an individual's positive or heroic impulses many psychologists study *unhealthy* individuals and thereby place undue focus on humanity's shadow side. While in the university, professors who taught Freud's theories upheld that emotions and impulses were dangerous. Wow, I thought to myself, religion and science actually *agree* on something. Freudian Psychology taught that unknown primitive aspects of me lay in the subconscious and unconscious ready to emerge should my ego lose control. The unconscious is believed to hold dangerous, repressed emotions and impulses just waiting to be unleashed, held in check only by the strength of the ego. Although we may scoff a Freud's sexual theories, few of us have escaped the above beliefs. That somehow at our core there lie "bad impulses, desires that need to be repressed or society will go rampant." Through my dance education, I have spent years unlearning a lot of what I was taught by these schools of thought.

Even if we manage to escape the negative influences of religious doctrine or mainstream psychological theories, most of us have nonetheless been exposed to the belief that: It is a dog-eat-dog world, and only the fittest survive. We may tell ourselves. "It is *mostly* about competition and

32

survival." Unfortunately, because we may erroneously believe we have to be tough to survive, we may lose our sense of joy along the way. But is life really mainly about survival? No, we were meant to do more than *survive*. Most Humanistic or Transpersonal Psychologics teach that we are basically good, our deepest impulses revolve around self-actualization, and thus we have a built-in impetus to *thrive*. There is so much more to life than just surviving or learning to cope.

After graduate school, I decided I wanted to do more than just survive, more than simply make ends meet—I wanted to dance through life! I wanted to thrive.

Is it any wonder that many of us are depressed and that the world is always at war? Many problems on our planet result from beliefs in the necessity of aggression and competition. On the extreme end, some of us may believe there is not enough of the pie to go around, we may believe only the conqueror or the tough competitor survives. Furthermore, because we presumably evolved from the apes, some of us assume our natures arc basically primitive and not to be trusted. Many scientists ignore the fact that nature and the animals are primarily cooperative and work to maintain harmony; so they rarely study the altruistic tendencies and heroic impulses of our own species. There are countless studies on the negative aspects of humanity, and plenty of news focusing on what's wrong with the world. There are few studies on the makeup of the healthy, self-actualized individual, or on what's *right* with the world. A simple shift of focus could steer the planet in a totally different direction.

It is not surprising then that many of us subconsciously distrust our basic human nature, feel unsafe in the world and believe the world filled with evil. If we can't trust others, or even our own impulses how can we enjoy simply being, let alone being with our fellow men and women?

Many women feel unsafe, uncomfortable with, or out of touch with, their femininity. As a youngster, I learned being feminine meant being weaker or a burden. I feared being feminine meant I was vulnerable and needing protection. This is what my father (who was a product of his culture) and the Church taught me. To be strong, I believed I had to minimize my femininity and act more like a man, ignoring my intuition, my sensitive nature, my ability to empathize, my own deeper feelings. This is what society taught me. I didn't believe I could be *simultaneously* strong and feminine.

**My Father Wanted a Boy**

Like many fathers, my father wanted a firstborn son. Because my mother is Danish, he also hoped for a child with blond hair, light skin and blue eyes. But, he had me, a first born daughter with dark hair, brown eyes and olive-skin. I suppose he accepted my dark hair and brown eyes, because my mother gave birth to my green eyed, lighter skinned sister a year later. However, while I was still living under the same roof, I don't think he ever quite accepted the fact that his first-born came out a *girl*.

This came to my attention when I was about sixteen. In a moment of anger, he exclaimed, "Why couldn't you have been born a boy, damn it?" He continued, "as long as you are a girl, you should stop showing anger because no man will want to marry you. You need to work on becoming sweeter, softer and more feminine, like your sister." Although shocked and deeply hurt, I managed to joke that I would be happy to undergo a sex change to fulfill his wish for a firstborn son. The sad think is, I was halfway serious.

Although I never became a tomboy, nor did I become sugar and spice and everything nice. I did grow up confused as to who and what I was. He apologized later, but the damage had been done. How does a woman who should have been a boy behave? Naturally, as a teenager, I experienced conflicting feelings about becoming a woman. After all, I was born a *girl*, and there was nothing I could do about it!

I wasn't sure it was safe or even good to be female. After all, my religion taught me it was Eve who ate the apple and manipulated Adam into doing the same. Thus, the Christian Bible insinuated that females are manipulative and weak. I also learned that girls are liabilities because they don't know how to take care of themselves and need protection.

To varying degrees, many of us are told it is not necessarily a positive thing, let alone a powerful thing, to be female. Subconsciously, we internalize the statement, "I am not okay." We are taught to hold ourselves back and repress our true feelings. And, repression often leads to depression. Not surprisingly, it is mainly women, not men, who suffer from depression. From my experience as a mental health counselor for ten years, many women suffer from mild to moderate depression for years and *don't even know it!*

Through the ancient and powerful art of belly dance, I slowly began reconnecting to the power and joy of being in my female body. I gradually reconnected to the strength inherent in my femininity. I came to realize the power in sensitivity. I couldn't be a good dancer without that sensitivity.

In our ancient past, it was not necessarily the tough guys who survived. On the contrary, it was often the sensitive individuals who were able to sense danger as well as other people's psychological states who were better able to adapt and survive.

Through belly dance, I learned to express my feelings and trust my sensitivity. It was incredibly healing to listen to the primeval drum rhythms of the Middle East. These ancient rhythms helped me connect to my body, especially to my hips and pelvis. Connecting to my lower body helped me to connect to my feelings of shame and guilt, and to then move them through my body. As I choreographed dances, I developed a keen ability to feel the mysterious music and to express my emotions.

Although both sexes possess these abilities, they are largely classified as female by society. Women are encouraged to develop these traits more often than men are, but they are not necessarily taught that these traits are naturally positive and powerful.

Through belly dancing, I began to experience the healing power of connecting to my feminine side. Slowly I began to realize these characteristics increased my sense of power! What's more, as I connected to my femininity, and to other women, I felt less alone and began to connect to a power greater than myself. I connected to my spirituality, the feminine aspect of the Divine. My joy for living began to return, and I began to feel alive again!

**The Monk and the Belly Dancer**

Jamie was in her early thirties and a student of mine. She called to tell me that she wanted to study belly dance because her teacher, a Buddhist monk, suggested it would be therapeutic. Incredibly open, Jamie explained that she did not feel comfortable being in her female body and often felt depressed. Part of her training to become a monk demanded that she connect to her female body and thus to her feminine power. Her Buddhist teacher required that she not only study but also *perform* a belly dance! What a wise teacher. He understood the healing power inherent in this ancient dance form.

When Jamie first came to my studio, it became obvious she felt more comfortable wearing unisex clothes and absolutely no makeup. She always wore baggy slacks, oversized shirts and possessed extremely short hair. Tall and extremely thin, I honestly couldn't tell whether she had any hips. It didn't take me long to realize Jamie came to me reluctantly, only to honor the advice of her Buddhist mentor. However, she left a few months later, transformed and ready to perform one of the most feminine dances in the world! She even gained some healthy female pounds and curves.

During the short three months she studied with me, I watched Jamie embrace her blossoming femininity. Although she kept her hair short, she eventually bought a long red wig and bought a beautiful two-piece belly dance costume. One night, she experimented with wearing a little makeup and a dress. I almost didn't recognize her. She looked beautiful! She appeared more whole. There is nothing wrong with a woman not wearing makeup or dresses, but this woman actually told me that she had a strong distaste for anything remotely considered feminine.

One night, she came to class wearing feature-enhancing makeup and a sexy dance costume. She let me know her mentor asked her to put on a show that weekend for her Buddhist group, and she felt "nervous as hell." Despite her nervousness, she performed that Saturday for her teachers and fellow students. Much to her complete surprise, she shared with me that she enjoyed expressing herself in this way. She thanked me and let me know that although difficult at first, she now enjoyed belly dancing and felt more sensual, feminine and alive. She had taken a *huge* step toward owning her sensuality as well as her sexuality.

Months later, I ran into Jamie at a supermarket. She explained that not owning her feminine side proved to be one of the biggest obstacles in her life not just in gaining monk-hood. She shared with me, "Once I acknowledged my femininity through belly dance, I completed my Buddhist training with flying colors. Not to mention, I took a giant step in my life as a whole."

**Belly Dance and Modern Culture**

Today in our post-industrial society, many of us are depressed because we feel isolated. Mother Teresa once stated, "Loneliness is the poverty of the West." We have forgotten the concept of the unified tribe. We have forgotten the truth in the old African proverb, "It takes a village to raise a child."

Today, in our post-industrial society, we have lost our connection to the Earth and her seasons, to the inner wisdom within us that says we are *more* than our bodies, more than our looks, more than our age, more than our weight. But, the earthy, repetitive drum rhythms of North Africa and the Middle East give us permission to reconnect to our bodies and to a distant past when human beings lived in tribes—close to nature, the animals, and to one another.

During my first year studying belly dance, I met two interesting and fun-loving women. Karen and Julia were two earthy women who exuded passion, sensuality, and fun. They became my friends as well as dance partners with whom I performed in several shows, including the California

State Fair, the Sacramento Library, and the Crocker Art Museum. Eventually, I joined a wonderful troupe and felt part of a dance tribe. Today, there is even a form of belly dancing called, "American Tribal Dance," which celebrates the unifying, tribal aspects of belly dance and, in particular, the *sisterhood* of the dance. Throughout my many years of dancing, I have been a member of five different dance troupes, including my own, "The Eye of the Cobra." Each offers its own unique interpretation of the joy of belly dance.

After graduating from UC Davis, I entered the work force, but continued belly dancing. As a mental health professional working with chronics, seriously emotionally disturbed clients, belly dancing was the way I maintained my *own* mental health. My colleagues claimed the sword I danced with served as a phallic symbol; they believed I danced for male attention and to work though sexual wounds. This was simply not true. Although, it was immensely therapeutic in working through my shyness, low self-esteem, and childhood grief, I primarily danced for the sheer joy of it!

Throughout my many years as a dancer, I came to the realization that the dance has always been within me, waiting to be unleashed. This is true for you, too, because the movements unfold naturally and easily. Today, in my forties, I am as active as ever, teaching and performing at countless shows. Thinking back to my childhood and adolescence, I find it amazing that I became a professional belly dancer. I was supposed to be a doctor, like my father. What's more, I was supposed to be a *boy*! It's no accident, I chose to pursue one of the most feminine and beautiful dances on the planet!

*Your Dance of Power*

Because belly dance is a very expressive dance, it can play a significant role in healing your past. We carry a myriad of repressed feelings in our bellies. When we dance, especially within the context of a group, we begin to release these feelings and replace them with joy. Furthermore, your power as a woman increases when you dance with or for a group of women.

The belly dance, as stated earlier, began as a dance created by women and danced for women who were giving birth. The belly dance has been passed down from mother to daughter for generations in the Middle East. Rarely, does a young girl attend a belly dance class in the Middle East; they simply don't exist. Most girls learn from the women in their own families. The dance traditionally began as a dance honoring female power and possibly as a prayer to the Goddess.

There exists tremendous power when women gather together. This is why I strongly encourage you, once you believe you have learned enough moves, to take an important step and dance at a student show. It is helpful to have a teacher. It is also very important you choose a group of healthy women to dance with. Many teachers hold open dancing for their student troupes, for other teacher's students and for solo dancers as well. These are like student recitals. There is no need to feel embarrassed because almost everyone is in the same boat as you. The audiences, usually belly dance fans, are incredibly attentive and supportive. Exactly what a beginning dancer needs.

## Performing to Build Confidence

During one of my first dance performances, I danced with a troupe at the California State Fair. To say I felt nervous is an understatement! We were dancing for a large crowd of complete strangers in over 100-degree weather. What's more, dancing to live drum music was a new experience for me. And to make matters even more nerve-racking, I had a major crush on the good-looking, lead drummer.

I danced the Turkish Karshlima with Karen and Julia. This dance is composed of a fast 9/8-dance rhythm with lots of jumps and turns. One *must* stay with the beat. The support of the troupe and my dance partners carried me through with flying colors. I am proud to say, we were a hit! Awestruck, our two male, college buddies stated that one day we would make our husbands very happy. I never forgot that statement. Today, I am married, and *I know* my husband is happy. After that show, I experienced a tremendous feeling of accomplishment. I became more confident, happy, and proud in other areas of my life as well. As a matter of fact, I asked that cute, dark-haired drummer out. He said yes! Feelings of confidence from a belly dance often transfer over to other areas of life.

Years later and hundreds of performances later, I became a dance instructor and eventually formed my own dance company. One of my talented troupe members, a young woman who started my classes at the age of twelve, is now dancing professionally. She is majoring in dance at the university, is a beautiful dancer and in great demand. When she was just fourteen she shared with me that belly dance had done more for her self-confidence than anything else in her life. Now, that is a powerful statement! Think about it.

Most students I speak with today experience similar feelings after their first student show. So take that giant dance leap forward and perform, even if it is just for your friends and family. You will be surprised at how appreciative they are and at what a great time you will all have. First, I suggest dancing with a group before going solo. But, there are always a few students who prefer performing solo because they don't have to worry about being on time with everyone else.

**Benefits You May Experience at a Student Show**

Just as with a teacher, it is important to dance with other students who are supportive and encouraging. So be sure to seek out other dancers like yourself who are on the path toward health and wholeness, who want to feel alive again. Below are some benefits you may experience at a student show, especially if you dance with other women.

1. If dancing with supportive women, you will feel a sense of *connection*, a sisterhood. You will feel a connection to the sensuality of your body.

2. You will begin to feel more comfortable in your less than perfect body. Although they may be, belly dancers do not have to be rail thin. Belly dance originated from an ancient, matriarchal era, when clans or tribes valued women for their rounded hips and bellies because it meant they were fertile. This was important to combat the depopulating forces of nature at the time.

3. In our society, we have been taught to cut ourselves off from our bodies and its feelings. You will begin to feel more unified with your body as you dance out your feelings. You will begin to like your

body and enjoy being in it. You will feel connected to its God-given sensuality and physical vitality. This will also aid in lifting depression and other emotional disorders.

4. You will impress yourself and others with your new skill. When you enjoy dancing, others will enjoy watching you, and you will feel a tremendous sense of pride in your accomplishment.

5. There was a time in our ancient past when our ancestors viewed our bellies as the sacred seat of life. Because you will be moving parts of your body others consider sexual or sexy, for example our hips and bellies, you will begin to unite with your body at a deeper level. Moving these parts in the presence of other women and feeling joy while doing so will afford you the opportunity to reframe your sexuality as *sacred*. This is where a great deal of your deeper healing will occur.

Society tends to sexualize belly dance. Unfortunately, it is difficult for many men to understand the sacred sensuality inherent in this dance form. This is why if your focus is on *healing*, it is important you perform with other women and in a largely female audience.

All of the above will be instrumental in alleviating depression and anxiety.

**Dance Exercises for Releasing Past Wounds**

If you are experiencing a serious and chronic depression, you may need *professional* help. None of these exercises are intended to substitute for professional therapy or to treat severe mood disorders such as chronic depression, bi-polar disorders or anxiety disorders. However, these exercises may be used in conjunction with a good therapist.

Belly dance helped me connect to the sensual and feeling aspects of life—feelings I was taught to repress by Catholic Schools, where I had to adhere to strict dress codes and strict rules. When we are stressed, depressed or feeling wounded, we tend to wallow in our pain or attempt to numb our pain through overeating, drinking, or other compulsive behaviors. One of the ways to work through feelings of grief and loss associated with most wounds is to express these feelings through movement. You don't have to be a great dancer to do this. Remember, the movements are so natural they are meant to unfold from within you.

### *Your Dance of Grief*

Done with the appropriate intent and focus, the following exercise is very powerful. You will begin to heal using your own made up dance movements. They don't have to look beautiful. You may use the belly dance movements you have already learned or any other dance movements. Also, with specific belly dance breathing techniques, you will begin to release the numbness, sadness, and anger associated with your pain. Slowly, you will begin to feel alive again as you begin to release your depression/anxiety. The breathing afterwards will begin to free your belly where most of us hold our feelings.

When my father died from lung cancer, I experienced most of the grief in my belly and heart area. I experienced stomachaches daily. One of the ways I worked through this was to place my hand on my belly and then on my heart as I moved to the music of my choosing. The music I chose helped me to release my grief. Placing my hand in specific areas assisted me in connecting to the feelings lodged in my body, and then I danced them out. Your body has a wisdom that your mind and emotions often lack; *listen* to your body's wisdom. Keep in mind that anger and other feelings are often aspects of grief or loss. For example, you may be angry because you lost something or someone, or because someone left you.

1. Make sure you are in a quiet room where you will not be disturbed and where you have enough space to move.
2. Choose music that moves you deeply, that allows you to feel whatever feeling is coming up: sadness, anger, guilt, etc.
3. Take a few deep, cleansing breaths.
4. Visualize the person or event that activated your grief.
5. As strong feelings begin to come up, ask yourself where in your body you feel them? It is often in the belly, heart, or throat area that we hold repressed emotions, but your emotions can lodge *anywhere* in your body.
6. Tell your body it is going to show you how to dance out the grief or other pain so that you begin to feel a release.
7. Place one or both hands on the area; if there is more than one area, choose just one to start.
8. Begin to move your body using pelvic lifts, drops, rolls, hip circles, hip accents, or figure-eights. Move your body in whatever manner feels appropriate or natural; trust in the healing capacity of your body. You may want to flutter or undulate your belly.

9. If you begin to cry, allow this to happen. If you begin to feel anger or some other emotion, stay with the feeling and continue dancing. Painful feelings often have many layers attached to them.

10. Continue dancing as long as you need to, or until your body simply says it is time to stop.

11. Slowly sit or lay down for a few moments, taking several deep breaths.

12. While placing your hand on the area chosen above as well as on the upper abdomen, engage in short, fast belly flutters or fast panting. This is an actual belly dance move. If you pull your tummy in as you exhale, your inhale should take care of itself. Continue for about three minutes, and then rest a moment. This will help you to release any remaining knots or anxiety that has accumulated in this area pertaining to your grief/pain. If more tears or anger come up, spontaneously allow for them.

13. Now engage in deep, slow, belly breaths, placing your hand gently on your abdomen as you feel it gently rising and falling with every inhale and exhale for about three minutes; this breath will bring you to a relaxed, more centered state.

At first, you may find yourself feeling worse as the strong feelings begin to release. This is the hard part of healing. Often, you have to *feel* it to heal it; and your mind and body need time to process these strong feelings. Be gentle with yourself as you begin to unfold your grief/pain. You may need to dance your pain out many times over the course of your healing. Be patient. Most people in our culture don't allow themselves to grieve long enough. Keep in mind that if you are depressed there is probably a real loss involved. The loss may be old, something you never healed in childhood, adolescence or young adulthood or it may be more recent. If your loss pertains to a divorce, a friend's death, or a death in the family, it may take as long as *one to three years* to complete the grieving process. However, dancing your feelings out will keep your body and mind clear and expedite the healing process.

### *Opening Your Heart Dance*

You need to fill your well regularly. Connecting to the joy inherent within you is also a part of the healing process. No matter how traumatic your life has been, you have experienced joy even if just for a few moments. Calling up your lost joy is paramount to healing. You will not feel whole simply by expressing painful feelings. Once you begin to empty out the pain within you, a well begins to form within you that you will then need to fill with vital energy. This vital energy is what my ancestors, the ancient shamans of Peru called, "aini." I think of it as the vitality of life, the dance of life. You need to fill the empty spaces within your heart with the positive and healthy "stuff "of life. So, don't dance primarily to express your pain or just to be sensual or for attention. Although these are OK reasons, belly dancing is most healing when you dance to reclaim your joyful place in the universe, even if you are just dancing in your messy living room!

1. Pick your favorite happy music. Find a quiet place where you won't be disturbed.

2. Remember a time in your past when you experienced a deep sense of joy and peace. If you don't believe you ever have, then in this present moment, *pretend* you know what peace and joy feel like and begin to experience them.

3. If possible, dance in your own sunlit backyard or in a park where you won't be disturbed. Otherwise, make sure there is plenty of light in the room you are in. And, I wasn't kidding about dancing in your living room.

4. Take a few deep, cleansing breaths.

5. Tell your body it knows how to feel joyful, that it knows how to express joy in motion. Tell yourself that you are going to begin to fill the empty well within you. Trust in the wisdom of your body.

6. Place your hand on your heart as you begin to listen to the joyful music.

7. Allow yourself to move your upper body with belly dance movements, such as ribcage lifts, drops, or circles. When you begin to feel the joy welling up within you, continue moving in any way that feels joyful, happy, and light to you. Shoulder rolls, shoulder shimmies, or shoulder accents are also wonderful ways to express the heartfelt emotion of joy and to activate the heart center. Do not worry about how the movements may look. Enjoy your body as it connects to the power of joy.

8. If you like, you can videotape and later view your dance when you need to fill your well more.

9. After your dance, sit down and breathe deeply for at least two minutes to ground and center your energy. You don't want to leave your

room dancing on cloud nine, especially if you have practical matters to attend to. However, you can carry that feeling of joy with you at a subtle, but powerful level.

### *Belly Breaths for Anxiety and Sleeplessness*

When I have difficulty sleeping, I first engage in the short, fast *breath of fire* (the belly flutters) for at least three minutes. Then for at least another three minutes, I do the slow, deep, belly breaths with my hands held in a prayer position over my chest. I find that the belly flutters soothe my anxiety, and the deep belly breaths then create a sense of calm within me. Before long, I am floating in the clouds and fast asleep.

### *Minimizing the Pain of Menstrual Cramps*

Belly flutters and belly rolls imitate birth contractions and so help expel the menstrual lining of the womb as they might expel a newborn infant. Step-by-step instruction in belly rolls is available in my first book, *Belly Dance Wisdom.*

### *Belly Dance Movements that Heal*

For those of you interested in taking a belly dance class, I suggest you ask your teacher for a private lesson to cover some of the highly therapeutic movements discussed in this section. For example, strong and fast movements like hip lifts, hip drops, shimmies, fast spins and head spins serve to release blocked energy.[6]

Belly dance instructor and performer, Atea, points out how many belly dance movements come out of ancient therapeutic dance traditions. For example, trance dances, also known as Zar dances, involve lots of head and body spinning. The Zar dance is an ancient ritual still used today in certain remote Egyptian villages to alter one's state of consciousness so as to heal a person with a mental illness who is often believed to be possessed. The repetitive Zar rhythm on the drum helps an individual focus her energy as she dances. This repetitive drumming starts out slowly, gradually building to a state of frenzy. The dancer becomes one with the music spinning slowly at first, then eventually spinning her body and head very quickly as the drum beat quickens. Eventually the dancer creates an altered state of consciousness in which she detaches from her body and mind. Finally, the dancer collapses from sheer exhaustion. This means the, "demons of negative energy have been released and peace and healing are enhanced."[7]

There exists a slow piece of music called the taxim (tak-seem), in which a solo instrument improvises a beautiful, slow melody. In another example of movements that heal, Atea states that hearing the taxim, "the dancer responds with circular, undulating, and soft movements of the torso, hips, arms, and head. These pleasurable motions harmonize the central nervous system, sending life-energy and mood enhancing hormones throughout the body. The mind becomes relaxed and centered. Through improvisation of movement, the dancer focuses on his or her creative response to the music. This focusing allows the dancer to be "in the moment." Altered states of consciousness may occur, leaving the dancer refreshed and recharged when the dance is over."[8]

# Healing Your Sexual Wounds

## Owning Your Wounds One Shimmy at a Time

I have spoken with several women who believe belly dance has been instrumental in healing their sexual wounds. They belly dance because it is sexually healing for them. Although I was never sexually abused as a child, as a young woman, I had a difficult time saying no to others, especially to men. I was taught to please people in general and men in particular. Like many women of my generation, my parents, schools, and religion simply never taught me that I had a right to my own body, to my own space, to my own feelings. There were several times I regretted that I didn't say no.

Sexual assault is more common than people realize. A study among college women has shown that 1 out of every 5 college-age women report being forced to have sexual intercourse.[9] Most childhood sexual abuse, nearly 85 percent is never reported.[10] Because of shame and stigma, many of these children won't deal with their trauma until they reach adulthood. Many *never* acknowledge they have been sexually abused.

Many women belly dance to find strength and power in their femininity and sexuality. These same women believe in the dance's power to heal sexual wounds. Here's what some of them had to say:

Lucy Lipschitz wrote for the Gilded Serpent Magazine, "To me, belly dancing is not about being cutesy and wearing bedlah (a belly dance costume). It can be so much more! I honor and respect all dancers; but others like me, who use this dance as a panacea for something personal, must also be given respect. We are seeing this dance help others to feel wonderful about themselves. We are using this dance to work some miracles."[11]

51

Daniela Gioseffi in *Earth Dancing* said, "One of our greatest enemies in the recent past has been the sexual repression brought about by patriarchal and puritanical ideologies. It is that sort of repressive hypocrisy that perverts true eroticism into smut, pushes the sacred over into the realm of the profane, and serves to defile the image of the ancient birth dance in the minds of many Americans."[12]

Massage therapist, Annamaria states, "Around my sexual identity, and response, there are many layers of numbness and shame, and yet I feel I am stripping away these layers through the movements of belly dance and increasing consciousness around these issues."[13]

## Connecting to "Sinful" Parts of Your Body

Through belly dance, I learned to connect to my body at a deeper level. I began to feel greater ownership of my body. When I danced, I felt I was inside my body, and I felt its power. I felt empowered because I was learning poise, grace, and balance. The more I danced, the more centered I became. But, even more importantly, I was connecting in a positive way to parts of my body that society had taught me were "dirty" or vulnerable to "sin." I was joyfully moving my belly, my hips, my pelvis, and my chest in a way I never had before—as representations of my feminine power and beauty. As I began to own and heal my wounds, I began to love being female.

Vicki, a very attractive student shared with me that she had been sexually abused as a child. Although she started belly dancing much later, when she was thirty-five years old, she found it helped her feel less vulnerable as a woman. She began to feel proud of her beautiful body, and she no longer felt she needed to hide her curves to feel safe. Furthermore, she felt the dance helped her maintain her self-respect because she learned to view belly dance as an art, as something beautiful and spiritual.

Another student, Janie, shared that since she could remember her father had sexually abused her. She explained that belly dancing helped her contact her power source, her belly. From that experience of power, she was able to connect to her environment and to others in a healthier way. She felt safer reaching out to others. Connecting to her belly power helped her begin to heal her feelings of shame.

I make it clear to my students that I teach belly dance as a sacred dance. How my students view belly dance is how they will then express the dance. I teach them that they have a choice. They can dance as women of power and beauty, or as glorified strippers aiming to please men. The choice is theirs. It is all simply a matter of focus and intent.

Belly dancing has the capacity to help you own your power and feel alive once again. If you have been repeatedly sexually abused or assaulted, you may have learned to dissociate from your body in order to escape pain. You may have also dissociated from the world. The result may be a state of numbness leading to an addiction or an unhealthy compulsion in order to feel alive again. You will find therapeutic power in belly dance because it allows you to begin to *feel* again. You begin to experience your natural passion and spontaneity once again. This helps you move away from your compulsions or addictions.

## Connecting to Your Sexual Power

As a belly dancer, I often feel I am a Rorshack Inkblot upon which others project their repressed or denied sexual impulses or problems. Because they have not owned their wounds, they project them out to the world. When I first began dancing, I had no idea how deeply belly dance may push people's buttons, especially their sexual wounds.

Over the years, I have learned to assess each crowd before I perform. I stay clear of any crowds or individuals who simply give me the creeps. I understand now that ironically, *they* are the ones with issues; it is not the belly dance itself. Like money, there is nothing inherently wrong or sleazy about belly dancing. I didn't learn to belly dance simply to be sexy or to attract attention. However, many women perform belly dance for these very reasons or worse, to act out their sexual wounds. For example, they may get into trouble acting out their sexual wounds by dancing primarily at bachelor parties, stripping at strip clubs or other similar settings.

In our society, healthy sexual expression is often blocked or expressed in a distorted shadow form. Belly dancing with the appropriate focus can be a means toward healthy sexual power and expression. But, as I have mentioned before, belly dance is so much more than about sexual expression. This is only one aspect of the dance. I began performing in order to proclaim my place in the universe. Today, I dance for the sheer joy and vitality it lends my soul. I know myself best when I am dancing. I realize sexual expression is simply one avenue the energy of the dance and my being can take. Of course, because our culture carries many distorted and unhealthy attitudes about sex and sexuality, this is usually the *only* aspect of belly dance the media and society emphasize.

**Too Much Talk, Not Enough Dance**

After ten years working as a therapist, I simply became fed up and quit. I was thirty-seven years old, burned out, and frankly disillusioned with many aspects of the mental health field. I met too many wounded healers, heard too much empty talk, and observed my colleagues place an overemphasis on illness and diagnoses. In the mental health profession, there is scarce research on *healthy* individuals and little focus on a client's strengths and healing capacities. It is rare to find studies focusing on mankind's heroic impulses or altruistic motives. The labels given to clients often serve to reinforce whatever disorder they are currently experiencing. For example, labels such as *victim* or *codependent* often serve to reinforce a weak and helpless self-image. From my experience there isn't enough focus on health and prevention. So, I turn to the art of dance.

Through my many years as a dancer and through my research, I now realize the therapeutic value inherent in belly dancing. I know this dance holds tremendous healing potential, especially for relatively healthy women who desire to own their feminine power.

I am not advocating belly dancing for seriously disordered individuals, but more as a self-help tool for women seeking a stronger sense of who they are. I know belly dance, danced in the appropriate context and with other women, can heal.

Despite its many postindustrial achievements, we live in a society that continues to devalue feminine traits and the female body. What better way to embrace one's feminine power, one's female body, and one's identity as a powerful woman than through the beautiful and sensual art of belly dancing?

After about ten years working in the mental health field, I decided I wanted to become a different type of therapist: a *belly dance* therapist. Today, I believe I am helping empower women more as a dance teacher, troupe director and performer than as a traditional therapist.   I have discovered that belly dance helps women connect to something deeper than their own words can describe.   What's more, it is a lot more fun than traditional talk therapy!

**How Belly Dance Can Heal Your Sexual Wounds**

From my professional experience as a therapist who has worked with both physically and sexually abused women and children, I believe belly dance has the capacity to heal your sexual wounds because it will help you to:

1. **Free the shame inherent in your negative body image.** Most of us dream of having a super slim body. And although it is perfectly OK for a belly dancer to be rail thin, the reality is that most belly dancers are round and curvaceous. The average professional belly dancer is probably twenty to thirty pounds heavier than the average ballerina. In the Middle East, to be curved and rounded is actually desirable! In Egypt today, famous dancers usually are curvaceous and have a belly. When I first started belly dancing, I was actually very slim.  I gained weight over the years belly dancing.  My husband tells me, "You look more like a woman now." However, most women dislike their bodies because they feel they are too heavy.  These same women feel right at home when they attend a belly dance class. They find it refreshing to see women perform who look more like them than ballerinas.

2.  **Reclaim passion and spontaneity in your life.** Because belly dance is very much an improvisational art and a solo dance, it will allow you to express your individual creativity. Creating your own dance choreography to music of your own choosing is cathartic and healing. Even if you only perform for yourself or close friends, it is powerful.

3.  **Validate and express your emotions**. This is crucial to healing your sexuality. As I mentioned before, belly dance is an emotionally expressive dance. Emotions exist for a reason, telling you something is wrong or needs to change. They are not simply vestiges of a primitive part of the brain. Anger often means your boundaries have been violated, sadness often means you need to grieve a loss, guilt often means there exists unfinished business in your life. The key is to listen and act upon your feelings *before* they build to the point of explosion. You need to honor all your feelings. Belly dance can be a wonderful outlet for these feelings. A few women I know dance solely for this reason.

You may carry a lot of repressed feelings in your belly. Privately connecting and releasing your feelings through belly rolls and other movements is highly therapeutic. As you begin to connect to your feelings, both positive and negative, you begin to feel alive again. You begin to feel safer and stronger.

When my father died, I choreographed five dances do express the different aspects of the grief I was experiencing. These dances depicted the five *universal* stages of grief. Eventually, I made the dances into a DVD.

Later, The Sacramento Channel aired these dances on television. Dancing out the feelings as well as viewing them later on TV was highly therapeutic. I received several calls from strangers who mentioned they felt a cathartic release simply viewing the dances on TV. One young man called me to mention he saw belly dancing as a beautiful, spiritual dance because it embodied the *Holy Spirit,* whom he believed was the feminine aspect of God. What a beautiful concept. I was touched! Years later, as I grieved other losses in my life, viewing these same dances once again proved therapeutic, cathartic and spiritually healing for me. If you would like to view these dances to better understand the grief process, you can purchase the DVD, Healing Dances for the Heart, at www.daleela.com

4. **Connect to your sensuality and then to your sexuality.** Many women, especially if they have been sexually traumatized, don't know how to be *sexual* in a healthy manner because they don't know how to connect to their bodies in a healthy, *sensual* manner. You must first begin to connect to your body in a sensual way by enjoying being in your body through movement, dance, and spontaneous self-expression. Once you begin to enjoy your natural *sensuality*, you will be well on your way to being your natural, healthy, *sexual* self. Because you will be connecting to your vitality and to the power within your body, you will then choose a sexual partner for all the *right* reasons. You will engage in sex to *share* your feminine power, beauty, and joy with someone you truly care about, rather than to give them away. Many individuals have sex to gain a feeling of aliveness, passion, or connection they lack rather than to express the aliveness,

passion, and sense of connection they already feel. They have sex because they feel empty rather than because they have something to give. Thus, they choose the wrong partners or simply *any* partner who temporarily makes them feel wanted or special.

5. **Create a foundation of power and strength in your life.** The basic stance of belly dance—bringing your feet close together, slightly bending your knees, relaxing your lower back, tucking your pelvis under, and engaging your buttocks, upper legs, and muscles of the pelvis—create a foundation of strength and free up old patterns of tension. As you engage in pelvic circles, pelvic rolls and belly rolls, your hips will shift into greater balance. You will feel the power alive in your body and a greater sense of connection to your body's inherent vitality. As you learn to connect to the earth through your feet and then raise the energy of the earth from your feet into your hips and pelvis you will gain power. Keeping your pelvis slightly tucked throughout the movements while isolating different body parts will teach you how to simultaneously control and relax your body. This relaxed but controlled state is transferable to your daily life. It is needed to successfully isolate belly dance movements as well as to function through the daily rigors of life.

Over a short period of time, energy will move more freely between your belly, hips, vagina, and perineum, the area between the anus and the vulva. If you have been sexually abused, you need to feel these places, especially if you have learned to numb or dissociate them from your body.

You also need to learn to move freely and fluidly. Belly dance will enable you to convey the essence of your femininity and to express yourself artistically. Ultimately, you will begin to experience increased energy and power in your entire being.

Rosina-Fawzia Al-Rawi in her wonderful book, *Grandmother's Secrets,* writes, "In essence, belly dancing is an art of loving. Like love play, it is a mixture of openness and reserve, excited tremor and endless lightness, a nearly unbearable intensity and a soft sensuality. Although it may appear tremendously wild to the onlooker, it also communicates a feeling of balance and inner peace, close to transparence and fragility, just like the arabesques and calligraphy of Islamic art."[14]

## Belly Dance Classes are Safe

I believe one of the most therapeutic actions you can take for yourself is to find a good belly dance teacher and class. Dancing with and even for other women is incredibly healing. It is extremely important that you feel comfortable with your teacher and the other students. Most women who have undergone sexual abuse need to find a compassionate and sensitive teacher. Remember, teachers are people too. Find one who matches your personality.

In reality, I don't know anyone who has ever made it *big* as a belly dancer in our culture. In the Middle East, dancers have become famous, legendary dancers, Tahia Karioka, and Samia Gamal became stars in Egyptian films. But, we have yet to see this phenomenon occur in the West. So if you have visions of dancing in a big Hollywood movie, beware. Even if you do receive a part, the dance parts are usually small or overly sexualized. They simply feed into the stereotype of the belly dancer as the dark, seductive, evil temptress.

I saw "Xena" the "Warrior Princess" belly dance once in one of her old TV episodes. Although this was one of my favorite TV shows, I was *not* impressed with this particular episode! Not only was she an amateur dancer, she used her seductive appeal to get to the bad guy and then *kill him*! Unfortunately, I have seen this image more than once portrayed by the media. In reality, this dance is a dance of *life,* honoring fertility and childbirth, not a dance of fatal attraction and death.

**Feeling Alive Again**

One of the quickest ways out of your feelings is to simply go *through* them. There is no shortcut. To repress negative feelings is not going to make them go away. Also, there is no magic cure for releasing trauma. The fastest way to get through traumatic memories is to go through them, reconnect to them, and then release them physically and emotionally through the body. No amount of talk therapy will compare. The energy of strong emotions often embeds in our bodies, muscles, bones, joints, indeed, in the very fiber of our being. We are affected on multiple levels by trauma, whether it is sexual or physical.

One of the best ways to connect to traumatic memories and feelings so you can then release them is through reconnecting to your body. When I worked as a psychology intern, a supervisor once told me, "A client often plays mind games, she may talk her way around her pain, she may choose to lie to herself about her feelings by repressing, minimizing, or denying them, but her *body* will never lie. So, watch her body language." I have never forgotten that gem of advice. Our life *is* imprinted indelibly in our bodies. And our bodies reflect how we feel on a daily basis. You can tell someone is depressed by the way she moves, by the tone of her voice, even if her words say otherwise.

A sexually abused woman will carry the trauma in her body, especially in her pelvis area. Until she acknowledges this fact, she can talk all she wants, and even fool her therapist, but she will never fool her body. Miriam, a beautiful belly dancer had been abused by her father since she was a small child. She said that part of what kept her sane throughout her insane childhood was going to her dance classes. As a child, she took modern dance. The freedom inherent in the music and dance helped her feel a measure of control and love for her body, even though it was being violated at home. She believes she may have literally gone crazy otherwise. Later in life, she also took belly dance lessons and felt the healing power of this dance. Because it was earthy and feminine she felt more connected to her body.

## One of the Sexiest Dances on the Planet

Belly dance, like American Modern dance, offers freedom of expression. Because it is one of the sexiest dances on the planet, it offers a fantastic opportunity to heal your sexual wounds. What better way to push all your sexual hang up buttons than through connecting to the sexuality of your body as you gyrate your hips, undulate your belly, and shimmy your shoulders. What a beautiful opportunity to heal.

If you have been violated sexually, you probably don't feel good about your body, especially about your pelvis, hips and belly. You may not feel in control of your body. You may feel guilt and shame about what happened to you. Are you blaming yourself? If you associate sex with pain, shame, or trauma, you may be having a difficult time being joyfully sexual. You may be sexually promiscuous as a way of acting out your pain, as a way of reliving what occurred to you in your past. Or, you could be sexually repressed. Until you cope with your past, you will continue to act out sexually or totally repress your sexuality. It is not uncommon to go to either extreme.

You hypnotize yourself into believing you will never have a normal life, a healthy relationship, or a dynamic sex life when you repeat detrimental things to yourself about your past, your present, and your future. You can hypnotize yourself *out* of this thinking through belly dance.

Belly dance is hypnotic. The soft, undulating, snakelike movements, coupled with the exotic, sensual North African rhythms, has the power to catapult you into an altered state—a state in which your senses come alive, and your body, mind, and soul live completely in the moment. You can discover the joy and beauty inherent in your body and feelings through the power and beauty of belly dance. You can begin to feel proud that you have hips, breasts, and a belly. You can feel beautiful even if you are overweight, over fifty, or *believe* you are ugly. You can begin to own your power even if you believe it was taken away from you long ago through a sexual assault.

**A Giant Dance Step toward Healing—Student Night**

One of the most powerful ways to value your body's natural female shape and enjoy being in it is by impressing yourself and others with your new skill by performing at a student night. Because this dance is so sensual, it has the capacity to heal your sexual wounds. Especially in the company of other women, connecting to the sacred sensuality of the body and belly instead of over-sexualizing it will enable you to be in control of your body. You will learn to create stronger boundaries.

A few of my students, who are now excellent performers, were victims of sexual abuse. They have told me that dancing in the company of other women or even solo for a primarily female audience is incredibly healing. This is because other women, who are also learning the dance, are empathetic. Some of them have also been sexually wounded. They understand the courage it takes to connect to the power of this dance. They understand the power of this dance as healer. Because you are healing body parts considered sexual, the dance becomes sacred.

I strongly encourage you to take that giant leap forward and dance at a student show or recital!

## Exercises for Feeling Sexually Alive for the First Time

Belly dancing requires a certain amount of letting go, of bodily freedom. It requires that you forget what society tells you about moving your pelvis, hips, and belly. It requires that you allow yourself to shamelessly become absorbed in your natural femininity. A shameless femininity will allow you to freely and joyfully embrace age-old movements, such as hip shimmies and belly rolls. In releasing your inhibitions and freeing up your pelvis and belly, you can find yourself again. You will connect to your naturally beautiful and dynamic sexual self.

## *Dancing in the Dark—Part I*

These exercises can be done alone or with someone you trust completely. Whatever it takes, it is most important that you find a time and place where you will not be disturbed and where you feel *very safe*. Part I, II, and III are best done in one continuous sitting, but this is not required.

1. Take a few cleansing breaths and allow your worries to subside. Tell yourself you can always worry later. Write these worries down if need be so you can focus on the present moment.

2. Tell yourself that your subconscious knows what you and your body need to work through. It also knows just what you are ready to face in healing your sexual wounds. Trust your subconscious and trust your body. Allow your daily worrisome, conscious mind to let go. Allow the part of you that knows what to do to lead you through this healing exercise.

3. Pick music that you find sensually appealing and beautiful. Most soft belly dance music has sensual appeal. Listen to it once with the lights very low. Lying down helps to evoke actual images.

4. Tell your body it is safe, and that it will remain safe throughout this exercise, no matter what memories come through.

5. Lie down and listen to the music. Allow whatever images your subconscious mind is showing you to surface. Maybe you will see yourself conversing with someone else or working on a project. Images of the person who hurt you may surface. You are completely safe now. Maybe you will simply feel peaceful and no images will come forth at all. Whatever happens, just follow your stream of consciousness and see what healing path it shows you.

6.  After the song is over, write down any important notes or insights.

### *Dancing Naked in the Dark—Part II*

1.  Play the music once again. This time see yourself dancing naked to the music. See your body engaging in hip circles first, then pelvic lifts and drops, and then belly rolls. These are all movements that connect you to your sensuality.
2.  Ask yourself, what does my body feel as it dances sensually, what does it need or even what strengths does it feel? You are using your visual brain to connect to your inner being as it expresses itself through dance.
3.  In your mind's eye, combine the above steps in any way you please. Make up your own sexy belly dance. Continue to see yourself dancing *naked.*

    This is not about looking beautiful and graceful as you move. It is about connecting to how your body feels as it begins to move parts considered sexy or shameful, as it begins to connect to memories of past sexual abuse or trauma.
4.  Take note of what comes up for you.

### *Dancing Naked in the Dark—Part III*

1.  Keep the lights low; or possibly light a couple of candles so the room is not completely dark. You should still be able to see sufficiently to dance around the room without bumping into anything.
2.  Tell yourself this time when you dance naked, it will be for *real.* You will dance a sacred belly dance with great joy and abandon. You can

even make it an offering to God, the Goddess, a higher power, or to your long-lost innocent inner child. You can make it an offering to the child within who never received the protection and love she needed and deserved. Believe you *can* do this. It is important in order to begin healing.

3. You have had practice doing this in your mind. Now take your clothes off and dance naked for real! Have fun! Dancing naked in the dark feels great; it is incredibly freeing!

4. Connect to the feel of your flesh as it moves. Pay close attention to your pelvis, hips, and belly as they gyrate and shake. Be sure to use hip circles, belly rolls, and pelvic movements. Tell these parts of your body that you honor and respect them, that you enjoy moving them.

5. Now allow them to move you! Don't think. Simply connect to the music and allow the music and your body to move you.

In doing this three-part exercise, you begin to release your pelvis and liberate your hips and belly. Subsequently, you free yourself from trauma at your own pace. You are taking a giant step toward owning your sensuality and sexuality.

There was a time in our ancient past when our ancestors viewed our bellies as the sacred seat of life. Because you are moving parts of your body that *are* sacred, and because you are doing this in your natural, naked state, you can joyfully unite with your body at a deep level. So what that the world considers this dance sexual. In truth, moving these parts and feeling joy while doing so affords you the wonderful opportunity to reframe your sexuality as sacred. This is where a lot of your deeper healing comes in.

### *The Mirror Exercise*

1. Stand in front of a full-length mirror, again naked.
2. Allow whatever criticisms or dislikes you possess about your body to surface.
3. Place your hand on each part of your body you are unhappy with one at a time and state:

> *I thank you for how hard you have worked for me, despite my ungratefulness.*
>
> *I apologize for all the times I have mistreated or abused you.*
>
> *I now allow you to be the best possible (insert the appropriate body part here, i.e. belly) you can be. I accept you just as you are.*

# How to Enliven Your Marriage

## (The X-rated Chapter)

### A Marriage between the Soul and the Flesh

Many people view belly dance as *primarily* sexual, when in reality it is a *marriage* between the spirit and the body. When people view your belly dance ONLY as sexy understandably you may become angry. This attitude renders you a one-dimensional being. But you know you are so much more and so is the belly dance!

It is important that your sexuality be a beautiful and sacred aspect of your married life. The need to be sensual and sexy is a natural and vital part of your being. But, after many years your relationship may have become boring and stale. Belly dance can be a powerful way to heal your marriage and spice things up. Your sexuality is an important and valuable aspect of your life and so you must nurture it in your relationship. The sensuality inherent in belly dance can be an important asset in this worthy endeavor.

Please keep in mind that this chapter is *not* about portraying yourself as an exotic dancer in *public* but about enlivening your marriage in *private*. I present these ideas to be utilized between two people who care about each other, in the *privacy* of their own homes.

### How You Can Be the Most Sensual Woman He Has Ever Known

Although it started out as a birth dance, belly dance is also about the power of feminine sexuality. This chapter is for you if your sex life has become boring and routine. With the powerful sensuality and eroticism inherent in belly dance, you can transform your sex life, but you must have a strong desire to do so! You must want your marriage to work.

Belly dance is a powerful way to spice things up. Even television projects this idea. Years ago, Fox Television aired an episode of the sitcom *Married with Children* in which Peggy, Al's bored housewife, attempts to entice him. After many years of marriage and two children, he is also bored and rarely pays attention to her. In an effort to get her husband's attention, Peggy enters a "sexiest woman" contest as a belly dancer. She enters the contest in disguise so her husband will have no idea he is watching his *wife* dance. It works! Al does not recognize his own wife because she hides her face behind a veil. She dances wearing a simple belly dance outfit, engages in a few simple belly dance moves, and not only does she win the contest but she also gains her husband's total admiration! Al is absolutely mesmerized!

You too, like Peggy, can mesmerize your husband or lover! Belly dancing is one of the sexiest art forms in the world! Although it started out as a birth dance, belly dance is also about the power of feminine sexuality. After all, think about it: pregnancy, birth, and sex are all related!

## Gaining Aphrodisiacal Powers

What is it about belly dance that lends it strong aphrodisiacal powers? The fact that it is a passionate gypsy dance, a sensual art danced primarily from the *soul* is its most powerful aphrodisiacal characteristic. Other aspects of the dance that render it an aphrodisiac include its accompanying hypnotic music and the contrast between the soft, snakelike undulations, and the sharp shimmies, and pelvic/hip movements. Furthermore, the dance is connected to nature and reflective of all that is feminine and soft.

The fact that it is often improvised and danced from one's *heart and soul* without a preset choreography is its most powerful appeal. Think about it? What could be more enticing than viewing someone you care about dance from his or her heart and soul just for *you?* Making someone feel *special* is the most powerful aphrodisiac in the world.

Even an amateur can use this aphrodisiac to spice up a stale twenty-year plus marriage or to enchant a brand new lover. In this X-rated chapter, I will share with you fifty ways to entrance and seduce your lover! Also, I will teach you how to mesmerize your lover with your own X-rated belly dance; no matter that you are an amateur dancer. All that matters is that you love your sacred body and dance from your heart and soul. Most men find a woman who enjoys being in her body and who exudes confidence sexier than a physically beautiful bombshell who constantly whines about her every little flaw. That gets old fast!

Another important point I would like to make before you set off to entice your lover is the importance of viewing sex as good, even sacred. This viewpoint is also a powerful aphrodisiac, unfortunately, one not often held in Western culture.

Love your female body, and he will too! If you have already read the previous chapters and taken up belly dancing, no doubt you already feel fitter and sexier than ever before. If your mate doesn't respond to your increased self-enjoyment and confidence, then maybe it's time to find a new lover...

Before you begin enticing your lover, remember that thousands of years of history are backing you up in this exciting endeavor.

**Sacred Lovemaking**

Sacred lovemaking originated around 2300 B.C and was practiced in the temples as a form of worship. Caste tribes from Algeria, like the Ouled Nayl, who were mainly comprised of dancers and performers, may have developed sacred lovemaking around this time.[15]

The Ouled Nayl, located in Central and Southeastern Algeria were Arab Bedouins who practiced a pagan religion predating Islam. Due to Frances' colonization of Algeria in the 1830's, their legendary dances and the dance-meanings have disappeared.[16] Nonetheless, remnants of these tribes still exist today.

The dancers of the Ouled Nayl were born into a tribe that highly valued the arts of the courtesan. From the age of thirteen, daughters of the tribe became dancers and courtesans in the cafes of many Algerian towns. Observes demonstrated their appreciation by showering the dancers with gold coins. The dancers then used these coins to decorate their costumes. After they reached their twenties, they returned to their tribal land to marry and become *respectable* wives and mothers. They never danced in public again.[17]

Included in the tribe were sacred temple priestesses of the Mother Goddess who acted as protectors of her divine sexuality.[18] Belly dance may have been a form of prayer in motion. When I dance alone, I often pretend I am one of these powerful temple priestesses, dancing a divine dance in honor of the Great Mother and in honor of the sacredness of my female sexuality. It works! I finish feeling energized and healed, ready to share my joy with my husband…if you know what I mean.

Many of our tribal ancestors once considered belly dance movements sacred because they viewed the hips, belly, and pelvis as the seat of life. Thus, tribal people used hip movements, belly rolls, and pelvic circles to represent the act of conception as well as birth. It is well known that indigenous women gave birth in a squatting position, undulating and rolling their bellies to delivery their babies.

Furthermore, many ancient cultures used belly dance type movements as a form of courtship, as a dance to attract the opposite sex. When I visited the land of my ancestors, Peru, I witnessed an exciting Afro-Peruvian courtship dance in which both male and female dancers danced with a six-inch long and two-inch wide strip of cloth sewn onto the back of their pants or skirts. They looked as if they had tails. Both sexes took turns attempting to light the other's *tail* on fire! The dance turned into a sort of game to see who could achieve this. It was both suspenseful and comical. For fun some of the dancers attempted to light the strips with lighters held by their teeth. Throughout the *entire* dance, both male and female dancers swung their hips strongly from side to side or up and down in order to challenge the other's lighting ability. I could not help but think of the American phrase, "Light my fire."

Strong hip movements reflecting the creative powers of women, and danced as a form of goddess worship or prayer also characterize the popular Hawaiian, Tahitian and Polynesian dances. An exuberant Flamenco dance called the Fandango originated as a courtship dance. The Zambra Mora, a Spanish dance with Moorish origins is more like belly dancing than Flamenco with its' lively hip movements. It is clear, these type of movements were an integral part of many culture's rituals. In many parts of the world, remnants of these ritual dances continue to exist as folk dances.

## How to Mesmerize & Tantalize Your Husband/Lover

### *Setting the Stage by Making Him Feel Special*

How do you light your lover's fire and become the sexiest woman he has ever known? There are sexual techniques and skills that can help you and your partner enliven each other in the bedroom. Although, we will focus on some of these physical techniques, it's more important to focus on psychological techniques. With regard to the latter, begin by changing the way you view your partner.

To be romantic and sexy is a decision. Romantic sex is where the sensual meets the sexual. Believe it or not, men like romance too! Romance is bigger than life; it sets the mood. When we add romance, we key up the senses with candles, chocolate or grapes, soft lights, a fire, rose petals on the bed, a gentle touch.[19]

Research at Stanford University supports the evidence that your brain is the center for sexual arousal.[20] Since your brain is the center for sexual arousal, when you change the way you view your partner, you can make an impact on his behavior. If you see your mate as unromantic, unenthusiastic, boring, stubborn, or tired, your mate will react to this and continue to be boring, unenthusiastic, and tired.

However, as you begin to treat your loved one as though he were sexy and romantic, you will undoubtedly reawaken the passion between the two of you. By telling him how sexy he is, how much you like different parts of his body, (men rarely get to hear this), and by doing small things to make him feel special, attractive, and alive, he will become more attracted to you because of the way you make him *feel.*

Before lovemaking, it is extremely important that your mate feel you love him just as he is in order for him to respond to you sexually and to make mad, passionate love to you. One of the first steps you need to take is to tell him you love him and think he is sexy just as he is, warts and all. It is much easier of course to criticize and nag him.

Dr. Ellen Friedman, author of a series of tapes on how to make your marriage more exciting, talks about focusing on what's *right* with him for a change, on his strengths, rather than weaknesses. Praise him daily! Chances are, he already knows what his faults are, so stop criticizing him; tell him how important he is to you instead.[21]

One of the ways to show him how important he is to you is by truly listening to him. For example, she says when you find yourself at home with him, take the time to ask him how his day went, and really listen for about thirty minutes. In this manner, you will be teaching him to do the same for you.

Another romantic idea is to write him a love note that includes five wonderful traits about him and tape it on the bathroom or car mirror so the first thing he sees in the morning is your love note telling him how wonderful he is.[22] Better communication is the pathway to intimacy and better sex.

Most psychologists point out that usually it is up to the woman to teach a man how to be more romantic and how to set the mood for lovemaking. This is because most men simply don't know how. No one ever taught them how to be romantic.

There is no such thing as a romantic relationship that just happens. Two people have to work at being romantic, at making love, and at making life more exciting. So, take the initiative. Teach your mate how to put the passion back into your lives. Belly dance is a powerful tool in this regard.

Dr Friedman also suggests a woman plan a surprise that will create a memory. Wow! What better way to create a memory than to use belly dance to enact some of his fantasies, as a role-play, and even as part of your sexual technique.

An aphrodisiac is often something different and fulfilling, something no one else has ever done for him, something mysterious and alluring. Below, I list fifty ways to set the mood and spice up your love life. Using your skills as a belly dancer, you can be the sexiest woman in the world to your lover.

I hope it is clear by now that being a seductive dancer is more than just about technique. It is an energy or aura that you exude when you dance for your lover. It is only common sense to refrain from using these techniques when dancing for the general public. It is important to portray yourself as an *artist t*o the public, not as a seductress. Portraying yourself as a dance seductress not only gives the dance a reputation, but it gives you one as well! As mentioned previously in the book, this dance is not about seduction.

However, there is a time and a place for everything! And if there is a time to be seductive with your belly dance, it is with your husband/lover in the privacy of your own home. At the end of this chapter, I give away my secrets on how to make your dance seductive as hell for your lover.

**Fifty Ways to Entice Your Lover**

Starting on the next page you will find a compilation of fifty fun ideas I have collected from other dancers, articles, experts throughout the years on how to use the aura and mystery of the belly dance to captivate your lover. I have elaborated on the first two to give you an idea of just how intricate you can make these fantasies. The rest you can keep as simple or make as fancy as your heart desires. I have not attempted all of these; fortunately my husband is very warm blooded. So please let me know how these work for you and your mate!

*Arabian Fantasies*

1. *From Your Secret Admirer*

What you will need: a new but simple belly dance costume. It can be as simple as a see-through veil wrapped around your body in a toga with a hip scarf around your hips or you can go all out and buy a fancy costume. It's up to you. Just be sure it is new to your *lover*!

Write your mate a letter in your own handwriting so he knows it's from you! You can place your perfume on it or a smudge of lipstick. Place the letter preferably in his mailbox at work. If this is not possible, place it in your home mailbox. Address the letter to him with no return name or address. In the letter, tell him you are his secret admirer and are going crazy just thinking about him. Tell him that it is about time you take action and finally speak with him.

Ask him to meet you in your favorite restaurant. Come dressed in a sexy belly dance outfit. One he has *never* seen before. Make sure you wear a long coat or sweater over the outfit so you don't get harassed before he arrives. Hopefully it isn't 100 degrees outside. When he shows up, act as though you don't know him. Most likely, he will play along. Then, allow flashes of your costume and skin to show through the coat, thus giving him enticing glimpses of your body and costume. Continue to talk to him as if you just met him and are indeed his secret admirer. Tell him you can't wait to go to a hotel room with him to show him the rest of your costume. Make sure you have hired a sitter ahead of time and reserved a hotel room.

2. *Beautiful Virgin Dancer*

What you will need: A cell phone and a home phone (or two cell phones) and a tranquil, mysterious setting.

One night after the children have gone to bed or are at a relative's house, as your partner watches TV or is otherwise occupied, call him from your cell phone. In your deepest voice, tell him that you are his psychic, Madame Sophie. Let him know you have just had an important psychic vision you must share with him: "You will meet a beautiful young virgin dancer tonight whom you will transform into a sexually fulfilled woman. As a matter of fact, she awaits you at this very moment in your bedroom."

We spend about a third of our lives in the bedroom, so create a tranquil environment beforehand, no work-related items here. Use soft lights, red light bulbs are great, several candles, romantic music, and soft textures like satin or silk. Throw a couple of chiffon veils over the furniture and over the bed's headboard and pillows.

Feng Shui states our surroundings have an effect on our emotional, spiritual, and physical well-being. So avoid cramped conditions, throw beautiful smelling rose petals on the bed. Light some incense, too. Now you have become his virgin dancer.

Feed him grapes, play erotic music, and, of course, belly dance for him wearing a sexy costume. Don't forget to act the part of the shy virgin. Tell him you want to learn all about love and that you couldn't have found a better teacher than him. Tell him, "Please be gentle." Remember what it was like to be a shy virgin?

Use your imagination and have fun! The nice thing about not being a true virgin is that you can have a heck of a lot more fun being a "virgin" the second time around. For many women, the first time was neither romantic nor fun.

Here are some other ideas to get your imagination rolling. The possibilities are endless. Use your own creative imagination to add to the following role-plays:

3. *The Egyptian Queen and Her Slave*

This time you can be the one in control and playfully order your lover to fulfill your every (reasonable) desire. For example, you can playfully spank him for being a bad boy or order him to spank you. Make this fantasy as elaborate or as simple as you like.

4.  *The Consort of the High Priestess/Dancer*

There is evidence that in prehistory high priestesses chose young men to act as their consorts for a year before these young men were then sacrificed to the Goddess. It was considered an honor to be a consort. As a high priestess/dancer, you have chosen your current lover to be your consort. In this fantasy, you can ask your male consort what his last request is before he is sacrificed the day after tomorrow!

5.  *Nature Lovers*

Use the power of the natural world to enhance your lovemaking. In ancient times, fertility, sexuality, and nature were connected. Because being outdoors heightens sensations, one of the most beautiful, healing acts is to make love in nature. Some of us have never made mad, passionate love under the stars, on the beach, or in the woods with the sun shining on our warm, naked bodies. It is important to find a private, comfortable, safe place during good weather.

Some ideas: on a warm summer night, swim in a lake together naked under the light of the full moon, or feed each other wholesome fruits, read each other poems with the birds singing, the sun shining, and the wind blowing in your hairs.[23]

## 6. Variations on Nature Lovers

Invite your lover to see you dance in your backyard. Imagine you are by the Nile Delta, basking in the warmth of the ancient Egyptian sun. Belly dance for him under the sun or moon while holding a platter of grapes. Feed your partner grapes as you seductively dance around him. Dance with or without clothes or do a playful striptease. Another variation is to have your costume on but leave your panties off! In the winter time how about renting a cabin for the weekend just for the two of you and dance for him by the fireplace. Any of these scenes will most definitely create a memory.

## 7. The Dance of the Seven Veils

You can wrap seven veils around your body in a myriad of ways. For example, one around your head like a turban, let another hang around your neck to the back, and the other also wrapped around you neck but hanging down your chest like a scarf. Two wrapped around your hips in opposite directions, another tucked in both bra straps and flowing down the back, the seventh one held gently in your hand. You can use beautiful light silk scarves or less expensive chiffon. A wonderful website to go to for gorgeous, hand-dyed silk scarves is www.akaisilks.com.

Now dance your own rendition of the seven veils to slow, hypnotic music. I love the songs, "Moon Dance" by Van Morrison, "Dancing in the Moonlight" By King Harvest, or "Moon River" by Henry Mancini. Pick your own, favorite, romantic music.

## 8. *The Arabian Princess*

As a royal princess, you can play the part of the tease. You are the beautiful, sexy princess, Arabia. Tell him he may look but not touch. For example, tie him up then caress yourself while he's tied up. He'll go crazy! Of course, don't forget to untie him when he's had enough.

## 9. *A Variation of the Arabian Princess*

He ties *you* up as *his* sex slave and you the Arabian Princess then pleasure him at his command, within reasonable limits of course. Use common sense and make clear to each other your limits.

## 10. *Your Genie: Three wishes*

This one is very similar to the one above. You are his genie and you grant him three sexual wishes. Don't forget to dress the part of a genie. Again, use common sense in how far you will both go.

## 11. *His Favorite Dish*

Cook him his favorite dish. Dance a little belly dance for him, then place the food in strategic places all over your body, and let him eat away! Make sure the food is not too hot or cold on your skin. Of course, you may also place the food on his body, and you can then eat him away.

## 12. *Take My Panties Off*

I heard this one from a friend: Shave your pubic hair in the shape of a heart. This will definitely surprise and delight him the next time he takes your panties off. As he discovers your secret, tell him the heart is a symbol of your love for him, and that, as a symbol of his love for you, you would like him to dance for you. You man wish to teach him a few belly dance moves first. Wouldn't it be nice if more men danced for *us* for a change?

## 13. *Belly Dancer Tattoo*

You can have a Henna artist do this so the tattoo is not permanent, unless you want a permanent tattoo. Have the artist place the tattoo on your buttocks and then surprise him during lovemaking. This will be a night he will always remember.

## 14. *Hot-Tubbing with Nerfetiti*

Take a look at some photos of Nefertiti and what she wore or what the ancient Egyptians wore, then go to a costume shop. Make your own costume or improvise. Invite him to go hot tubbing with you. Surprise him by coming out dressed as Nefertiti. Bring some music with you and dance an Egyptian belly dance for him before ending your dance with a striptease just for him.

## 15.  A Belly Dance for You!

This is more involved than number ten. Tell him it is one of your fantasies to see him belly dance for you! Who says your man can't look sexy belly dancing? Make him a gift certificate stating he gets a free one hour *private* lesson on how to belly dance. Encourage him to belly dance for you after his lesson by telling him you think his body is sexy, and you can't wait to see him dance for you. Promise him you won't laugh. On the contrary, tell him you would just go mad with passion if he danced for you and you alone, even if just for one minute! Easy moves to teach him are: hip circles and backward figure-eights as well as simple baby shimmies.

## 16.  His Sex-Ed Teacher

This is a variation on the above. Dress as a sexy belly dance teacher. Don't have sex! Make him wait until he has mastered a couple of belly dance moves. Start by teaching him a few belly dance moves, then tell him you are going to also teach him how to rediscover kissing, holding, touching, and just exploring each other. As hard as it may be; don't have sex. This will make your next lovemaking session that much richer and exciting. Remember, he is your student, and as a good student, he must listen to his teacher.

### 17.  Belly Dance Naked

Light the whole room with as many candles as you can find.  Mist the room with rose fragrance.  Play your favorite sexy music.  My personal pick is, "You Give Me Fever" Sung by Peggy Lee or by Ray Charles with Natalie Cole. Come out completely naked and begin undulating. Need I say more!

### 18.  Belly Dancer Biker Chick

After the hustle and bustle of the day, tape a note on the bathroom mirror where you know he will see it before he goes to bed or on his car mirror in the morning. The note should say something like, "You are looking at the sexiest man on earth. Tonight, come and join the sexiest woman on earth for a fun-filled wild night in the bedroom." Give him a specific time.

That night, when he enters the bedroom, be dressed in a black leather jacket with a black leather mini-skirt or tight, leather pants and black high-heeled boots. Belly dance in this outfit before you take it all off for him!

### 19.  Unveil Me

This is a variation of the seven-veil dance.  Wrap yourself in as many veils or scarves as you can afford: ten, twenty, and even thirty.  Tell him you are an Arabian beauty queen, but the only way he can have you is to unwrap you one veil at a time. To challenge him further, tell him before un-wrapping each veil, he must say something flattering about you. Tell him flattery will get him *anywhere* he wants.

## 20. *Famous Belly Dancer*

Your name is Yasmine. You are the most famous belly dancer on Earth, and you are going to do a private dance just for him alone! Dress the part! Look like what he thinks a famous dancer would look like: very glamorous with exotic eye makeup, high heels, and a colorful, ornate costume. Tease him with your dance; don't be in a hurry to bring your partner to orgasm. Most of the fun is in teasing him.

## 21. *Playboy Photographer—Part I*

What you will need: a camera with plenty of film. Tell your husband he is a famous playboy photographer who is going to photograph the sexiest belly dancer in the world. You! Get him to photograph you in as many *risqué* belly dance outfits as he can. Using a self-timing camera, why not ask him to join you in the photo?

*22. Playboy Photographer—Part II: Belly Dance Calendar*

Choose the twelve best photos and make a *Belly Dancer Babe* calendar for him. You can take the photos to most photo shops, and they can do this for you, especially around the holidays. You may give it to him for no reason other than to spice up your love lives or save the calendar to give to him as a special gift for the New Year. Below and on the next few pages are a few sexy ideas. Please, please, don't dress like this in a public show! For his eyes only!

### 23. His Very Own Special Fantasy

Ask him what is his idea of a fantasy dancer and then use common sense acting it out.

### 24. Fantasy Harem Girl

Your lover is a king with his own harem, and you are his favorite. Dress up your bedroom to look like a Hollywood Harem. Place plenty of pillows on the floor to sit on, drape veils over tables and other furniture, place a bowl of grapes by the bed, and use red light bulbs for soft lighting. Use your imagination and play the part of his favorite Fantasy Harem Girl. Treat him like the king that he is.

### *Using Tantric Sex to Lead Your Lover to Bliss*

Tantric sex is about connecting to something greater than your self through sexual union with another. Unlike many avenues to healing, Tantra is one of the few paths that views sex as sacred and as a means to unite with the Divine Power. It is about realizing our unity with the "Almighty" and with all life; it is about healing through sex.

Here are several suggestions on how to begin to move toward blissful sex. Not all of these will suit all partners. Some of these suggestions may seem a little "touchy-feely" for a man. Don't force him. Ask him to try it just this once for fun and adventure. If he doesn't like it, you can always try another suggestion.

## 25.  Read about the Art of Sexual Ecstasy Together

It can be very erotic and exciting to read about the art of ecstatic and blissful sex together.  I recommend you and your partner read, "The Art of Sexual Ecstasy," by Margo Anand.

## 26.  Hold Positive Beliefs about Your Sexuality

If you think you hold negative ideas or hang ups about sex, here are some positive beliefs you may wish to adopt: You deserve pleasure. Sex is not simply a genital affair. Sex is good and is about sharing your love or caring with another. There is no right or wrong way to make love. Sex is about intimacy and not just meant for procreation. You are not dependent upon your partner for orgasm or sexual fulfillment.[24]

## 27.  Heart Salutation

Use the following Eastern salutation to begin and end lovemaking sessions: Sit naked.  Face your partner and gaze gently into each other's eyes.  As you inhale, bring the palms of your hands together in a prayer position in front of your heart.  Together, close your eyes, and as you exhale, bend forward from the waist until your foreheads lightly touch. Feel the connection between you. Then sit up, open your eyes, look into your partner's eyes, and say, "I honor the God/Goddess within you." Your partner reciprocates. Feel the reverence for each other this greeting conveys.[25]

## 28. *Create a Sacred Space*

This is important for lovemaking. You can do so by following the principles of Feng Shui outlined earlier and by creating a ceremony to dedicate the space. When you create a sacred space you feel protected and supported in transforming your sexuality. This creates a distinct break from daily life. It can be as simple as tidying up the room and lighting candles to walking counterclockwise around the space three times to dispel negative energies.[26] For a distinctly Arabian atmosphere, you can create a tent-like space with beautiful, ornate pillows.

## 29. *Sensory-Awakening Ritual*

Take turns introducing a wide range of sensations that are beyond ordinary life. The active partner blindfolds his lover. I have adapted Margo Amand's ritual to reflect the belly dance theme: starting with the sense of smell, choose different essential oils such as mint or orange blossom for your partner to smell. You may use instruments such as finger cymbals, tambourines, or a drum for enhancing the sense of hearing, a piece of silk or a feather for touching your partner in erotic places. You may feed him foods such as grapes, baklava, and grape leaves to taste. Finally, slowly take off his blindfold. Look into each other's eyes in silence. This can be a deep experience. Then he shares his experience verbally. Wait a day or two before exchanging roles.[27]

## 30.  Seductive Belly Dances

Take turns dancing seductively for one another other.  See the end of this chapter for the seven secrets to a seductive belly dance. I recommend you begin, since women tend to feel more comfortable dancing. Your partner gives his undivided attention to your dance.  Dance for at least five minutes expressing your love for your partner. I suggest you enact a beautiful belly dance as the Goddess Isis and your mate may then choose to enact another Egyptian God. Each in turn becomes a god/goddess. Your partner will not join in or touch you as he watches, but will simply take in your energy and essence. When his turn arrives, don't despair if your partner is reticent. Not all of these suggestions will suit everyone. Many men have never danced for *anyone* and may find this too intimate.

## 31.  Honoring the Ancient Earth Goddess

Belly dance began as an ancient ritual honoring fertility, pregnancy and childbirth. As a woman you have a powerful, ancient spiritual tradition to draw from. Create a sacred ritual in which the two of you honor your fertility, *or your* nurturing and intuitive abilities if you don't or can't have children.

Your lover will offer you a small gift to demonstrate his respect and reverence for the Divine Feminine energy residing within you. For example, he may choose to buy you a beautiful, not necessarily expensive, moon pendant. Other ancient symbols of femininity include goddess figurines such as Isis, cats, water, butterflies, doves, the beauty of nature and roses.

As he gives you his gift he will state in his own words: "I appreciate you as the embodiment of Mother Earth, as the embodiment of the feminine principle that gives life and nurturance to all living things." A woman does not have to be fertile nor have children for this statement to apply. Women often play nurturing and caring roles in society through their jobs, toward friends, parents, and lovers. Most metaphysical bookstores sell jewelry or other similar tokens representing the feminine.

### 32. *Honoring the Divine Masculine Principle*

It may be that early man did not understand the connection between sex and childbirth, that men carried the seed to create life. Fortunately, our ancestors eventually came to understand the important role male fertility played in procreation.

In this ritual, you will honor your man with a nice gift representing the masculine in positive terms. Ancient symbols of male fertility and strength include the oxen, bull, rams, stags, horses and the sun. Again, any metaphysical store can assist you in finding such relics in pendant or other forms. As you present your gift, state in your own words something akin to, "I honor you as the embodiment of the divine masculine principle that acts as the initiator of events and as a strong, protective force in the world."

*33. Learn About Advanced Tantric Sex Together*

If you are interested in *advanced* Tantric Sex, I highly recommend Margo Anand's book. Some practices you may learn in more advanced forms of Tantra are:

a. How to generate sexual arousal and channel the energy from the genital area to other parts of the body.

b. How to open the secret channel that connects all the energy centers between your sex center and your brain.

c. How to harmonize your inner man and woman.

d. How to awaken the ecstatic response.

e. How to expand orgasm.

f. How to go from orgasm to ecstasy.

g. How to circulate the energy of arousal through the secret channel together with your partner, thus creating an ecstatic circle of orgasmic energy.

Through an advanced posture of sexual union, you may create a state of bliss that takes you beyond technique into pure ecstasy.[28]

***XXX-Rated Ways to Captivate Your Lover*** *(For Adults Only)*

Although not all of the following techniques are directly related to belly dance, my general purpose is to help you discover your beautiful, female sexuality with your partner. Belly dance will encourage your confidence to try any of these suggestions.

### 34. Finger Belly Dancing

Very light, feathery touches can be more powerful than a regular touch or stroke. As you touch each other, realize that your entire body is an instrument for pleasure. To deepen arousal and to eroticize the entire body, not just the genitals, take turns finger dancing on each other's bodies. Be sure to look into your lover's eyes as you both breathe deeply. Focus; don't allow your mind to wander. Ever so lightly trace *figure-eights* around the breasts. This creates trust, especially for women. Draw *circles* around your partner's stomach with light, feathery strokes. Warm up the legs and arms with a deeper massage. Massage the hands and feet where reflex points connect to the major organs of the body.[29]

### 35. Love Brush

Take a brush and brush it on key love points: the side of the neck, the center of the breastbone, under the breast, between the navel and pubic bone, and along the center of the thigh. These are sensitive and erotic areas on the body.[30]

### 36. Stimulate the Clitoris, Nipples, and Lips Simultaneously

Don't just focus on the clitoris. Stimulating the clitoris, the lips of the mouth, and nipples at the same time creates sexual energy between these points that will convey arousal throughout the entire body. They are all connected.[31]

## 37. *Playful Tie Up or Spanking Games*

Dress him up as a dancing slave or vice versa. Take turns. If you want to be released, you can always say the word.

## 38. *Switch Sexes!*

You be the man, he becomes the woman. Then make love to him the way you would like him to love you and vice versa. You will be surprised at the insights you can gain with this one. Of course, with genital love, you will have to use your imaginations and talk out what you are doing or feeling as a man/woman. For example, tell your partner, "I am now lightly gliding over your clitoris," or pretend his penis is a small clitoris and treat it accordingly. Likewise as he strokes your clitoris as the woman, he can let you know he is now stroking your long and hard penis with his fingers or mouth. You get the picture!

## Seven Secrets to a Seductive Belly Dance

### 39. *Pick Exotic, Sexy Music*

The music you select sets the tone. Music that makes you feel sexy works best! Choose two songs that are about two to three minutes long each. Any more than ten minutes total may be overkill. Believe me four to six minutes of dancing will feel long when you are the one dancing! Pick one piece of music that is hypnotic and sultry and another piece with a strong, vibrant rhythm. Keep in mind that most men are *visually* stimulated so a beautiful dancer in a beautiful costume will set the mood fairly quickly. Pick his favorite music and costume. It will mean the world to him that you were so thoughtful!

### 40. Use Belly Dance Moves

Use the beautiful, sensual movements you learned in class. Begin with slow music. Dance with snake arms, undulations, figure-eights, and hip circles, and then for the second song, choose a strong drum beat and dance with stronger, accented isolations, such as hip lifts, hip drops, pelvic and ribcage lifts, shoulder accents, and more. You can also find all these moves in my first book, *Belly Dance Wisdom*, with step-by-step instructions and photos. The more you practice the more fluid and beautiful your movements will appear. Remember: anything worth learning takes patience and practice, or most women you know would be belly dancing!

## 41. *Love Your Body*

As you dance, outline your body with hovering hands. Follow the curves of your silhouette but never *touch* your body in a *public* show! For his eyes only. Love your body by outlining it with sensual touches. This is very

enticing and alluring in a dance. Try this in different dance positions. Begin outlining your body from your head, down either side of your body, continuing down the right leg and foot. Move back up the right leg (see photo) up your sides, place your left leg in front of you at this point and go back down the body to the left leg and back up. Men love a woman who feels

comfortable in her body. This movement is about embracing your body.

## 42. Dance with Confidence

Never mind your physical flaws. Your partner has them, too, and besides, he already knows your flaws. Let him see the *beauty and power* of who you are for a change. Move your body with your heart and soul. He will feel special and become mesmerized by the new you!

## 43. Use Plenty of Eye Contact

Belly dance possesses hypnotic qualities. As you gaze seductively at your partner, use repetitive, soft movements, one movement flowing into the other. For example, go from dancing hip circles to figure eights. You will create a trance-like atmosphere. All the while, look at your lover with a look of sheer joy and love in your eyes to enhance the power of this dance and to put your lover into a trance. You will draw him into your aura. You are letting him know he is yours for the night and that *you are in charge!* Most men love when a woman takes charge for a change.

## 44. Flirt with Your Neck and Hair

Legendary Egyptian dancers flirt with their neck and hair as part of their dance. I bet you don't realize how sexy you can look flirting with your neck. How? Roll your neck in a circle as you dance, or look to one side as you bring your hands under your hair (see photo) or just circle

your neck back as you caress your hair. As you lift your shoulder up, look at one shoulder with a turned chin, then look at him coyly, and smile alluringly at him. To look as if you are enjoying your sensuality is important; *this is at the core of a woman's sex appeal.* Play with your hair. If it is long enough, place your hands under it and pull it off your shoulders. If your hair is short, buy a long wig and surprise him.

*45, The Power of the Veil*
Come out with a veil wrapped around your body. Dance close to him. Slowly take the veil off your body. Dance with the veil using the beautiful veil movements from class or from my first book. See veil photo

Daleela Morad

106

Toward the end of your dance, place the veil around your man's neck or waist and pull him toward you (see photo). You may also place both of you under the veil as you seductively dance with him. This will create a strong feeling of romance and intimacy.

*46. Invite Him to Dance with You*

As you dance for him, playfully invite him to dance *with* you. If he tries to emulate your moves simply enjoy his efforts. He will probably look adorable just trying! Don't turn this into a class. If you do succeed in teaching him how to dance hip circles, undulations, or shimmies, an added benefit is he can use these during penetration for an enhanced lovemaking session.

## *Sexual Technique*

A *few* important notes on sexual technique:

47.  Slow down and breathe deeply.  Slow, relaxed movements are the key to Tantric lovemaking.

48.  Use a small pillow under your pelvis for greater penetration.

49.  The "doggie style" position best stimulates your G-spot.

50.  It is often easier to create female orgasms with the man on top while you raise your legs straight up.  This causes his penis to rub against your clitoris.[32]

## *Belly Dance Artist or Dancing Diva?*

These fun and new ideas are meant to bring you and your partner closer together. They are *sacred* enactments meant to increase your confidence as a person and as a lover.  Never portray yourself as a seductress in *public*! You will only be desecrating a beautiful art and putting yourself in jeopardy. A belly dance artist chooses to be an artist in public and a dancing diva at home; and then *only* for that special someone. You have a choice. There is power in your choice!

# Belly Dance—Goddess Dance

## The Goddess Dancing
### *Reclaiming the Sacred Feminine*

Lost under the veil of civilization's darkness
We search for our ancient temples
Hand and hand with our sacred flames we go
Eternal fire lighting our weary path

Despite the confusing maze of modern day life
We find one another and,
Together we reclaim our bodies
And our souls
Our spirits dance our female creative power,
And our souls remember:
We are the ancient ones
We are the Goddess

## The Story of Women

If you are interested in pursuing belly dance as an art, hobby or therapy I strongly encourage you to also learn about the Divine Feminine, the feminine face of God. Although this chapter is not directly about belly dance, I write this chapter because in learning about the history of women and the concept of the Divine Feminine, you will understand belly dance's esoteric aspects and ultimately come to a greater appreciation of your own sacred origins. This of course will add depth to your dancing, and will be immensely therapeutic for your life in general.

The more I studied and researched the ancient goddess religions and the sacred feminine, the more I appreciated the power of my femininity and the power of the belly dance. Through my newly developed talent, belly dance, I found a means to express this newfound power and joy in being a woman. Belly dance then became more than just a fun way to express my self; it became a spiritual path, a means to connecting more deeply to the Great Goddess Herself.

## Belly Dance as a Rite of Passage

When I first embarked upon my dance path, I was a nineteen-year-old university student. I simply wanted to learn that "cool" dance for fun and exercise. Little did I know I had just stepped onto a path that would become life transforming! I had no idea I was connecting to an ancient lineage with a rich history dating back thousands of years. At the end of this chapter, I will offer you a powerful visualization to connect to the power of the Goddess. You will joyfully learn how to channel Her healing energies through your dance, both for yourself and others.

In our post-industrial societies we have lost our connection to nature, to the Divine Feminine, and we are sorely lacking the concept of a global, unified tribe. Today in our nuclear era, most societies worship technology and the *conqueror*. But, through the beautiful art of belly dancing, we have the opportunity to revere the *nurturer*, to connect to the natural world, to uplift the value of the feminine, to unite Arab and American cultures, and to honor the phases of our lives as women.

Before Greek and Roman times, both men and women revered nature and the nurturer. In early times, through powerful rites of passage, both sexes entered the different phases of life in a powerful and meaningful manner. With the belly dance, you too can honor and celebrate the different phases of your life and celebrate the power and beauty of the feminine aspect of the Creator. At the end of this chapter, I will offer you exercises and guidelines to do just that.

You will also find yourself in a beautiful and sacred temple in our ancient past where as a tribal woman, you will enact and celebrate the *present* stage of your life through belly dance. No matter what phase of life you are in, you will use the magic of ritual to honor yourself. The vitality of youth, the advent of menstruation and womanhood, the miracle of motherhood, the pains and sufferings of your life, and the wisdom that midlife and old age bring are all important aspects of life to be celebrated. Today in our post-industrial world, we lack these rites of passage to mark the different stages of our lives.

Like many other forms of ethnic dance, the belly dance possesses a rich cultural heritage. It began as tribal ritual, transformed into folk art, and finally became artistic entertainment. It also has the capacity to act as a spiritual path to increase wholeness. Belly dancing can offer you an escape from the purely rational—a creative vessel for your ideas—and it can help you reclaim the sacred feminine. The more I connect to this art form, the deeper it dances its way into my psyche, slowly uncovering layers of wounding regarding my devalued femininity.

Thousands of years ago, dance was a part of spiritual ritual, and spirituality was a part of everyday life. Our ancestors remained connected to the Earth and lived peacefully amidst nature. They noticed that everything around them occurred in cycles of birth, life, death, and then rebirth. They observed this cyclical pattern in the phases of the moon, the bearing of fruits, the four seasons, and the rising and setting of the sun. They felt at one with nature; they regarded the Earth as sacred, as their living, breathing mother. Because women possess the magical power to nourish and bring forth life, it is not surprising that our ancestors conceived of their source as a Mother Goddess. It is also no surprise that our ancestors especially revered pregnant women.

This dance began as a communal event during a period in history when men and women lived in unified tribes and related in a more egalitarian manner. Tribal people danced to celebrate the seasons of nature, to connect to the animals, to celebrate the hunt or the harvest, and as rites of passage into courtship, pregnancy, and childbirth. Men and women lived side by side in a society that respected both the male and female aspects of humanity.

**God the Mother**

The most powerful gift this dance form presented to me was the concept of the Divine Feminine, or God the Mother. Due to my love for belly dance and due to my desire to connect to the value of the feminine, I began to research the sacred feminine and the ancient goddess religions. Books by Merlin Stone, Dr. Jean Bolen, Dr. Pinkola Estes, and Daniela Geoseffi opened my eyes to the possibility that, once upon a time, women were revered and valued for their femininity, for their rounded hips and abdomens, and for their power to give birth. I was pleasantly surprised to discover that from the Upper Paleolithic Age, about 25,000 B.C., archaeologists discovered some of the earliest representations of female fertility figures, which many scholars believe to be representations of a feminine deity.[33]

Human beings did not always live in a world that worshipped the god of the heavens as "God the Father." On the contrary, I discovered that for thousands of years, before the dawn of Greek and Roman civilizations, our ancestors once worshipped *God the Mother*. As I continued my research, I realized there existed evidence that many of our so-called pagan ancestors may have actually believed in *one* creator, and thought of God as "Mother."

**Belly Dance as Sacred Ritual**

In her fascinating book, *The Path of the Priestess: A Guidebook for Awakening the Divine Feminine*, Sharron Rose points out that temple priestesses were trained in the sixty-four sacred arts, including dance. Initiated into the feminine mysteries, young girls underwent years of arduous physical, artistic, and intellectual training, as well as intensive personal reflection. Throughout their training, they learned that each movement, gesture, expression and posture held deep meaning; ultimately, these dancers trained to become emissaries of divine energy, the embodiments of the Divine Feminine, and a means through which others could connect to the energy of the Goddess.[34]

Many of the movements of the belly dance also contain deep esoteric meaning. Understanding the meaning of these movements may assist you in connecting to the Divine Feminine. It is believed many of these movements originated from imitating the animals and other aspects of nature. In imitating nature, our ancestors believed they would take on the powers of that animal or natural force. The hip circle may be a representation of the moon or the sun, the half hip circle a symbol of the crescent moon, hand waves may reflect the waves of a river or ocean, the backbend may be a reenactment of a reed bending in the Nile, the figure of eight which is well known as the sign of infinity, may represent a woman's menstrual cycle. Finally, the serpentine body and belly undulations as well as snake arms so popular in belly dance very likely reflect our ancestors reverence for snakes.

Many teachers don't know about these connections. So, be sure you make these connections for yourself when you dance the above movements. You will find yourself relating more deeply to nature and to yourself through the beautiful, earthy movements of the belly dance.

## Dance Priestess—Connecting to the Goddess through Sacred Sex

At first, I was dumbfounded to read that from the earliest times in the Middle East, temple priestesses worshipped a divine female creator by having sexual relations with *strangers.* This was not considered prostitution. Payment was not made to the women themselves but was offered to the Goddess, and in return, men were allowed to take part in Her sacred rites. Through sex with these women, the men connected to the Divine Feminine.

In our ancient past, tribal fertility rituals frequently ended in copulation. Sex was sacred because it counteracted the depopulating forces of nature. Sexual energy tainted by a sense of sin and guilt developed later along with male-centered religions and patriarchy.[35] Today, our inability to connect the physical to the spiritual results in difficulty believing that sexuality was once an integral part of our ancestor's spirituality.

The belly dance is reminiscent of these earlier sacred rites, not only as a ritual birth dance, but also as a dance meant to educate virgin brides about sex.   Daniela Geoseffi points out that in the Middle East, the Awalem, literally translated as, "those who teach," were dancers hired to attend weddings for the purpose of hinting, stimulating, or initiating the bride and groom into the pleasures of the marriage bed.   Geoseffi states they were well-educated women versed in the arts, especially music, song, poetry, and dance. They often became wealthy dancing for weddings and other special occasions throughout Egypt. In Egypt today, the Awalem continue to dance for weddings in Cairo and other Egyptian cities. In the West, having a belly dancer perform at wedding celebrations originated from the Awalem.[36]

**Dancing on Cloud Nine - A Wedding in Egypt**

As a dancer, traveling to mystical Egypt to perform was a life-long ambition. I dreamt of being a part of the *Awalem* tradition before this tradition became lost in time. I also had fantasies of dancing for wealthy Egyptian families and coming back home with thousands of dollars in my pocket. What professional belly dancer hasn't? A gal has a right to dream doesn't she?

In November of 1998, I finally encountered the opportunity to visit Egypt, the *motherland of the belly dance*. Me and my dance companion, Layla, spent two exciting weeks touring Cairo, including shopping for costumes galore, watching the famous dancer, *Dina,* perform at *Le Meridian Hotel* and dining on a five-star cruise ship.

Our first night at the *Victoria Hotel*, we befriended the talkative telephone operator, Ahmed. A slim, talkative man in his early 30's, he spoke excellent English and proved to be a great conversationalist. Like many of the Egyptian men, he took an immediate interest in Layla with her long, thick, blond hair and penetrating blue eyes. In no time he proposed to her, she jokingly accepted, and we all became fast friends.

The entire hotel staff demonstrated great intrigue when we nonchalantly introduced ourselves as *Daleela, and Layla*. Even the hotel owner delighted in the fact that two American tourists held distinctly Arab names. Finally, he mustered the courage to ask us, "Why you use Arab names when you from America?"

Although we had planned to keep our dance status quiet, we decided to share our secret with him and the hotel staff. "We are dancers from the United States," we proudly stated, "And belly dancers from the United States customarily take on Arab stage names."

"Huh?" They eyed us quizzically, but smiled and nodded warmly nonetheless.

On our fifth evening in the lobby of the hotel, we had the pleasure of watching men dance for us for a change! In Egypt, everyone belly dances, even men. Ahmed and the male waiter from the hotel bar were no exception. What's more, they loved to perform in front of an audience. Right there in the lobby of the old *Victoria Hotel*, they performed the *Tahtib Stick Dance* for us. This is a male combat dance, possibly one of the oldest forms of martial arts, which originated in *Saidi*, a city in Upper Egypt. Their dancing thoroughly mesmerized us. It was refreshing to see men dancing for women for a change! And, they taught us a few new moves.

Impressed with our dancing skills, the next day Ahmed in perfect English said, "I would like to extend to you an invitation to perform at my cousin's wedding this weekend." Little did we know that the night before we had auditioned for a wedding show!

As a rank amateur, Layla hesitated to accept his invitation. I looked at her incredulously and asked, "But, how can you resist this rare opportunity to perform at an authentic Egyptian wedding, first hand? Isn't this is every belly dancer's dream?" It didn't take long to convince her to accept our new friend's generous invitation.

Saturday evening, Ahmed picked us up in an old, beat up black and white taxi with no speedometer or seatbelts. He introduced his soft-spoken friend, who acted as my escort. Unfortunately, my escort's name escapes me because he rarely spoke, since he knew little English.

Ahmed assured us his cousin had tons of money and the wedding would be "a nice one" with several hundred people in attendance. Wow! Were my fantasies of returning to the US with thousands of dollars in my pocket about to come true?

After a harrowing ride, the taxi finally slowed to a screeching halt. We expected to find ourselves in a beautiful five-star hotel. Alas, no! These gallant men escorted us onto a back street alley, squeezed between two dilapidated apartment buildings! The air smelled of dirt, the floor lay covered with multi-colored sawdust, and wet laundry hung high upon several apartment clotheslines, waving at us in the wind. Nonetheless, we found several hundred guests dressed in their "Sunday" best. The men and women sat divided on either side of the alley.

As we eagerly anticipated the arrival of the bride and groom, Ahmed introduced us to several guests, all of whom warmly stated, "Welcome to Egypt. Egypt is your home now."

Finally, the groom and his shapely, dark-haired bride made their grand entrance. Ahmed casually, but proudly pointed out, "The bride is his second wife."

"You mean he's already married!" I exclaimed, utterly dumbfounded. *Gulp...poor gal.* At first, the bride held her mouth taut, appearing quite serious for such a joyful celebration. I wondered what was going on in her mind and in her heart. I whispered to Layla, "Do you think she's met his first wife? Do you think his first wife is in the crowd?"

"I don't know," she answered, "But, if she is watching her husband marry *another* woman, this is just a little too weird for me." I nodded in agreement.

Like a regal queen, the beautiful bride walked in with her chin held high and her dark, oval eyes surveying the crowd in front of her. She nodded and smiled politely at the guests as she marched in time to the music, arm and arm with her new husband.

"She is beautiful and despite the serious look in her eyes appears warm and kind," I said to Ahmed, "What is her name?"

Ahmed smiled and his eyes sparkled as we watched her. "Her name is, Karima, and it means generous. She is a beautiful and kind woman in many ways. She gives much food and money to the poor every year during Ramadan."

Karima wore a gorgeous red evening gown. She mesmerized us with her large, brown Egyptian eyes, and her long, dark hair arranged high on her head. She looked in our direction, opened her mouth and flashed her straight white teeth at us. As she and her groom continued their gallant march down the saw-dusted path towards their respective seats, the men and women clapped in time to the Egyptian wedding march called the *Zafa*.

Suddenly, Ahmed brought Layla in front of the wedding couple. With wide eyes and a beaming smile, she danced with her arms held high for the bride and groom. The dance only lasted a few seconds, but this was enough to engage the crowd. She ended her wedding dance with a deep back bend as her curly, blond hair flowed like gold silk towards the dusty floor. The crowd watched mesmerized. Most of them had never seen a blond beauty who could belly dance!

Ahmed and his buddy quickly took us to one of the run-down apartment buildings to change into our dance costumes. They introduced us to a nice Egyptian woman who couldn't speak a word of English. She smiled graciously and gesturing emphatically led us to the second floor to a cold stone flat to change. After we changed into our red and gold beaded bras and belts with red chiffon skirts, we covered our bodies with long silk veils and headed downstairs toward the wedding reception.

Awaiting us below, Ahmed and my escort, his name still escapes me, immediately took a firm hold of our hands and led us quickly toward the stage. Suddenly, they began to run, dragging us behind them. We had no choice but to follow them. Alarmed, I wondered, *why the hell are they in such a hurry*? Within seconds I understood. The crowd, made up of two hundred plus men, women and children, began to surround us! The mob followed us all the way to the stage and began to encircle us, as Ahmed and my escort extended their arms to keep them at bay. My heart skipped wildly. This was getting a bit scary!

What's more, the stage stood *over* eight feet tall, wobbled under the band's weight and did not have any attached stairs! "How in the hell are we going to climb up on that thing without our two-paneled skirts flying open?" I screamed over the loud music at Layla.

Layla raised her eyebrows, sighed and stared at me, "Now I understand what big TV stars go through. Maybe we should just forget this whole thing."

Fortunately, our brave escorts had a simple but effective solution. They carefully but quickly hoisted us up onto the stage with their bare hands, as the musicians on the stage pulled us up. *Great teamwork.*

Whew! Finally on stage and safe from our admiring fans, we met the lively five-man band. I was pleasantly taken aback by their youthful, handsome looks as they asked us in broken English, "What music you want us play for you?" We asked them to play the number one hit song in the Arab world at the time, and our favorite as well, "Habibi Ya Nour El Aini" by Amr Diab.

As the band began playing this lively Egyptian piece, we danced together as a duet. After only a few minutes, a young boy, about thirteen years old, who had been dancing at the foot of the stage, hoisted himself up onto the stage and began to dance with me. He belly danced as skillfully and gracefully as any woman, or any adult for that matter. As she shimmied, another young man joined Layla and moved his hips. Toward the end of our show, a young woman in her early twenties came up and joined us as well. She danced *beladi* style which is a style of belly dance in which the knees are more bent, the arms are used less and the focus is on larger hip movements. This in contrast to the more contained, movements we were demonstrating.

And, the crowd below also danced along with us! Typical of Arab weddings, our belly dance had become a joyful, communal event in which everyone joined in and celebrated by belly dancing.

After our debut, our escorts carried us off the stage and dashed us off even quicker than they had brought us in because the crowd began to *run* after us. But, our brave escorts safely pulled us through. I was proud of them!

Unfortunately, Layla began to curse wildly at them as they pulled us up the apartment staircase. "Get your fucking hands off me. I'm not one of your Arab wives!" Alas, the poor woman thought they were kidnapping us!

As she continued to shout profanities at them, I quickly grabbed her arm and yelled, "Layla! Don't you see, they are only trying to protect us from our over exuberant fans!"

Finally, understanding their well-meaning intentions, she opened her eyes wide and then looked down at the stairs. "Oh how embarrassing," she said shaking her head, "What a blessing that no one understands American curse words!"

"Let's hope not," I sighed.

Oh, the images that may run through a tourist's mind when under duress in a foreign land!

Although we performed on an old rickety stage, in an outdoor alley, on rainbow colored sawdust, we had danced on *cloud nine*! I came to realize that in Egypt, a wedding is simply not a wedding without a belly dancer. Although I didn't come home with thousands of dollars in my wallet, what I came home with was priceless! I had been a part of the dying, but all-important tradition of the *Awalem*.

## Dance of the Magdalene & the Virgin Mary

I was profoundly moved to learn about the possibility that Mary Magdalene may have been a ritual dancer. Iris Stewart, in her book, *Sacred Woman, Sacred Dance,* points out that in 15th century France, a ceremonial dance called "Marie Magdaleine" was still performed on Easter Monday recounting the meeting of Mary and Jesus after his resurrection. Eventually, the Church threatened severe penalties for the continuation of this ancient custom and so the people turned it into a hymn called "Hail, Festal Day." Also, the nuns of Villaceaux in France celebrated the feasts of the Holy Innocents and of Mary Magdalene with ritual dances.[37]

Even more surprising, I discovered there is a legendary gospel that was written around 150 C.E. This gospel states the Virgin Mary may have also been a dancing priestess. Iris Stewart explains that the Virgin's mother, Anna, in gratitude to God for giving her a child, dedicated Mary to the temple at age three. In the temple, the child Mary danced for the joy of God, until the Levites required her to stop at age 12, lest she defile the ministry. This story was accepted by the East but discarded by the West. However, it reappeared later in the West during the Renaissance under the title *Protevangelium.*[38]

As a young woman growing up within the Catholic tradition, I was awed by the tremendous reverence my Peruvian grandmother held for the Virgin Mary. Although she only spoke Spanish, I sensed the incredible devotion my grandmother held for "La Madre de Dios," asking her for strength and compassion. As a paraplegic, the last twenty-five years of my grandmother's life were difficult, and she found deep comfort and solace in praying to "Santa Maria."

My grandmother loved to dance as a young woman. I heard many grand stories from my grandfather of her dancing on tabletops in her younger years. I smiled at the possibility that the sacred woman she had held in such reverence may have also loved to dance. Why would dancing make Mother Mary any less holy, I wondered? I looked to the work of Carl Jung for answers.

## The Archetype of the Dark Temptress

On occasion when I perform, I take on other people's shadow projections—usually their unacknowledged dark selves. Carl Jung coined the term *shadow* as the personification of that part of human possibility, (both negative and *positive*) which we may deny in ourselves and project onto others. As a belly dancer, I often feel I am a Rorshach Inkblot (a well-known projective personality assessment technique) upon which others project their sexually repressed hang-ups and fears.

One evening, I performed at a local Mediterranean restaurant. As always, in the tradition of the dance, I worked hard to involve the audience, women as well as men. In this particular establishment, I recognized Joe, a young musician I had performed with on several occasions. He recognized me also. As I performed, I smiled at him and casually invited him to dance with me. He sat with his tall, good-looking male *friend*. Little did I realize his male friend was in reality his *lover*. As we danced, I noticed a mean scowl on his lover's face, so I invited him to join us as well, but he only became angrier. Soon after, he stood up, sneered at Joe, and angrily stormed off. My dance partner quickly followed him out of the restaurant. Well, that put a different slant to "getting the crowd going."

As a professional belly dancer, I never know how the general public is going to react to my shows. No matter how beautiful the choreography, costuming, or how much heart I put into my dance, there will always be someone who misinterprets what the dance is about. I know I was not interested in anything else but dancing with this gentleman acquaintance. His partner however, only saw me as a threat to their relationship. Ironically, although I have had this type of sexual fear projected upon me by women, I never imagined a gay man would choose to react in this manner. In time, I finally realized negative reactions from an individual are rarely about me or about belly dance per se, but more likely about that individual; that person is revealing his or her unacknowledged hang-ups and fears, his or her unacknowledged *shadow*.

Over time, society has projected its fear of the dark temptress onto dancers in general. Women as dark seductresses appear time and time again in history and myth: Eve, Salome, Delilah, Jezebel, even Mata Hari in the 20th century. The belly dancer as the sexual temptress falls strongly into this category. The *dark temptress* is an archetype, a primal form of thought or experience that all human beings share in their collective unconscious.

According to the Christian Bible, it was a woman's curiosity and desire for knowledge that led humanity to fall from grace and perfection. She seduced the man to fall and thus became the evil seductress. Now nature and the female body became forces to be mastered. Many religions saw humanity's natural desire to experience the divine energy of sexual union as a dark, sinful urge to be repressed.

It took a long time for the ancient esteem in which women and dancers had been held to give way to the fear of female sexuality and the fear of women's power. In order for us to feel whole again, we need to own our shadows; we need to acknowledge the dark temptress within all of us and reclaim her as sacred. Belly Dancing is a wonderful way to do this. It is a way to honor our magical, feminine powers and revere our sexuality as sacred. Only then may we transform the archetype of the dark temptress into the archetype of the "Black Madonna," the black, fertile Earth Goddess who may act as a source of spiritual wisdom.[39]

**The Wild Woman**

Jungian analyst, Clarissa Pinkola Estes, has written about another archetype: the wild woman archetype. Unlike most of us who live in a success-oriented, materialistic society, the wild woman is in touch with her creative nature. In her book, *Women Who Run with the Wolves*, Dr. Estes describes the wild woman as that part of us in touch with our basic instincts, creativity, and freedom; wild does not mean out of control but natural. She explains: a wild woman is like a wolf—instinctual, intuitive, and playful; she knows her territory and how to set her boundaries. Also, she is loyal to herself and her pack and does not try to be everything to everyone.[40]

Unfortunately, when I worked as a therapist, I counseled many women who repressed this natural, healthy aspect of themselves in order to please others. Many of these women turned to alcohol or drug abuse. Beaten by their spouses or molested as children, they were no longer in touch with their physical, emotional, and spiritual wisdom. They did not know how to listen to their bodies and feelings, let alone heed the wise wild woman within.

Before the fall of the sacred feminine, women lived their lives in tune with their feminine instincts, intuitions, and their need to heal and nurture *themselves* as well as others. They existed aware of the connection between their menstrual cycle and the lunar cycle. One of my dance teachers, Majida Magdalena, calls this being *in tune with the moon.* They also lived in sync with their natural creativity and playfulness. Today, through belly dancing, we may begin to reclaim the wild woman within us!

## The Fall of the Goddess

The fall of the goddess religions and the destruction of anything resembling the sacred feminine or goddess worship struck a deep chord within me. This dissonant and solemn chord led me to a deep desire to understand why. Why was it so threatening to my ancestors to witness goddess worship? Why the gradual and brutal manner in which patriarchy came to be the usual order of things?

Through my studies, I learned that according to historians, scholars, and feminist writers who have followed the trail of the Goddess, our ancestors very likely worshipped a matrifocal, peaceful goddess 5,000 to 25,000 years before the rise of male-oriented religions. This egalitarian culture was destroyed by Indo-European groups of invaders. This did not occur overnight; it took many centuries, possibly several millennia for these invaders to destroy and eventually eliminate the last traces of goddess temples and goddess worship representing the powers of women. So why did our ancestors demolish these goddess worshiping societies? I decided fear was most likely at the root of this takeover, fear of women's power and fear of their sexuality.

Through their superior military skills, the Indo-European invaders violently subjugated peaceful goddess-worshipping cultures, imposed their beliefs, and subsequently fragmented the Great Goddess into many lesser goddesses. In, *The Holy Book of Women's Mysteries*, the author expounds that eventually the invaders completely imposed their patriarchal culture and religion on the conquered peoples so there was little trace of the Goddess left.[41]

According to the documentary, *Goddess Remembered*, these tribes imposed their male-dominated hierarchy and the worship of their sky gods on goddess cultures wherever they settled. By 1500 BC, earthquakes, volcanoes, and armed invasions by Indo-Europeans buried the last great goddess cultures in old Europe, the near East, and the Mediterranean.[42]

The suppression and eventual destruction of the Great Goddess, begun by the Indo-European invaders, was later completed by the early Hebrew, Christian, and Moslem religions. In order to take over, the emerging religions of Christianity and Islam needed to destroy goddess worship.[43] Wendy Buonaventura, points out this may be why these religions suppressed female dance connected to honoring female sexuality and fertility, and may explain why we find so little mention of women dancing in the Bible. Finally, as the Great Goddess fell from her throne, the male deity and men became the focus of these assimilated cultures.[44] By the time of the Roman Empire, dance was transformed from sacred ritual to mere entertainment for the Romans, performed by paid professionals and imported slaves.[45]

It came to my attention that the history of women and the Divine Feminine reflects the history of the belly dance. Belly dance also began as a sacred ritual dance but is now more often seen as sexy entertainment. As long as we do not honor all that is considered female within *both* men and women, how can we possibly honor women or the belly dance? The belly dance reflects all that is quintessentially feminine: softness, roundness, creativity, earthiness, intuition, sensuality, and emotional expression. These are attributes we as a society and as individual men and women tend to devalue in ourselves. It should then come as no surprise that we as a society devalue the belly dancer.

## Love-Priestesses

From 1540 to 1677, the word "prostitute" originally meant, "to offer with complete devotion or self-negation."[46] It was interesting to discover how today, the word "prostitute" distorts the original meaning of the ancient customs the word was meant to describe. It appeared to me that many ancient customs connected to the feminine have been distorted by the dominant culture in this manner. By the 1700's, the word "prostitute" meant, "given over or devoted to something evil."[47]

In India, The Devadasis were women once revered as sacred servants to Hindu deities. They often became the concubines of wealthy Brahmins or landowners in ancient India, but were considered *married* to the deities. They were possibly remnants of ancient priestesses who danced and sang to the gods and goddesses revered at the time. As concubines, they were valued by their lovers for their powers to connect them to their sacred deities. They were in essence *love priestesses,* but by the mid-nineteenth century they were labeled *prostitutes*. Tibetan Buddhists call these women dakinis. Dakini is a Sanskrit word meaning, "sky dancer". They are considered the embodiments of the Divine Feminine.

The word prostitute developed from female initiatory rites of passage into womanhood; these rites began with a period of isolation and instruction, leading to dances, songs, ritual baths, and body paintings, finally culminating in the public rite of presenting the girl to the community as a woman.[48]

These rites reflected the role of a young woman as creator and may have been the basis of the Eleusinian and other mystery schools. The Eleusinian Mysteries were annual initiation ceremonies for the cult of Demeter and Persephone based at Eleusis in ancient Greece.[49] Other mystery schools include the schools of ancient Egypt and its early kings. These schools taught great secrets about creation and the earliest civilization.[50]

Over several centuries, the feminine aspect of the divine became associated with destruction, sin, and death. Today, the Divine Feminine reflects society's shadow—that part of ourselves we do not accept or even realize exists. Women lost their sacred status centuries ago and are still often seen as temptresses of the flesh. The story of Eve in Genesis as the temptress reflects the negative transformation of the Divine Feminine to that of fallen woman. Also, we no longer revere the pregnant woman who *gives* life; we revere the conquering warrior, who *takes* life.

Belly dancing has the capacity to heal and transform us from many of these wounding beliefs. Beliefs so embedded in our culture we often don't realize they exist; they are so cleverly hidden. Belly Dance is about reclaiming our powers of creativity, and our roles as creators and spiritual leaders. It is about revering the natural woman, the pregnant woman, female sexuality and the Divine Feminine.

When I was only five years old, my parents told me the reason suffering exists in the world is because Adam and Eve ate the apple. Even at that tender age this line of reasoning made little sense. I protested, "Why do we *all* have to suffer just because Eve ate the apple? Why would a loving God

131

punish *me* for something someone else did?" The answer the Church gave me went something like, "The sins of the fathers are passed down to their children". What's more, the priests at the parochial schools I attended made it clear Eve ate the apple *first* because she is the weaker and less educated sex. A biblical movie pointed out that because of what Eve did God chose to punish her female descendents through the *pain* of childbirth.

When I gave birth to my daughter I felt intense power and joy; the pain didn't matter. I connected to all women before me who had experienced the same miraculous event. I connected to the power of belly dance as a birth dance honoring women as creators. As a result of giving birth, I released the concept of the fallen woman and embraced the concept of the Divine Feminine embodied in all women! I certainly did not feel God punished me by giving me birth pangs.

The repression and eventual elimination of the ancient goddess religions reached its violent heights between the 15th and 17th century with the appearance of the Inquisition and the witch craze. Many women continued to practice their old traditions, despite the possibility of imprisonment or even death.

**The Burning Times**

A very powerful and moving documentary film, *The Burning Times*, opened my eyes to the horrors of the historical period between the 15th and 17th centuries—the witch craze—and left a *profound* impact on me. This film opens with a powerful statement: "Long after Roman times, women continued the ancient traditions of the old religion with a thousand small ceremonies in their daily lives. They were leaders, counselors, visionaries, and healers. In Europe, their villages knew them as wise women. The Christian Church and State branded them witches and condemned them as worshippers of the devil. Their history once lost is being reclaimed by a new generation of women."[51]

This informative documentary outlines how the Church of Rome set up the Inquisition which had the power to execute anyone accused of heresy for something as simple as calling up the spirits of the Rhine. It is believed that eighty-five percent killed for the crime of witchcraft were woman. Between the 15th and 17th century, millions of women were burned at the stake all over Europe. The film further points out this may be called a *woman's holocaust*, a holocaust we are never told about! A high estimate of up to nine million people over a period of three hundred years, including men and children, but mostly women, may have been killed for the crime of witchcraft or heresy.[52]

It became clear to me that the Inquisition destroyed a way of life that had existed peacefully for thousands of years. "The victims took with them the stories and traditions of their pagan ancestors; nevertheless, we still call the Earth our Mother, a memory from the goddess traditions of our pagan past."[53]

## History is Written by the Winners

Why did I have to wait until I was in my mid-thirties to discover this? Why hadn't my mother, sister, girlfriends, or my school teachers and university professors taught me about the women's holocaust as a young woman? How different my childhood may have been had a parent or teacher taught me that, at one time, women were the original healers and counselors.

They were natural spiritual leaders, visionaries, wise women, midwives, and herbalists. How healing it would have been for me to hear that at one time, fathers *revered* their first-born daughters.

I eventually came to the realization I was never told about this aspect of history because no one I knew had been told about this either, including my mother and teachers! As the film pointed out, "history is written by the winners," and it is all about power. I learned not to blame men per se, because this is not about men but about the devaluing of the feminine within both men and women. From my experience, many women devalue the feminine as much as men, although they may be more covert about it. What many of us don't realize is that in devaluing the feminine, both men and women are devaluing very powerful and important attributes within themselves and society. *All* of humanity is suffering as a result.

Sharron Rose in her book, *The Path of the Priestess*, movingly states, "Do you remember any truly powerful female role model presented to you when you were a child? Do you remember any stories in which the dominant theme was what could be accomplished through the mutual support, companionship, insight, and imagination of women working together, uniting their energy and vitality?"[54]

Most of the stories (and history) I learned growing up exclusively glorified the achievements of men. I admired certain women, but it was mostly because they succeeded by acting like men. Because their cultures devalued their feminine power, many of these women had to deny much of their feminine natures in order to make it to the top.

There is a battle going on within each of us regarding the lack of balance between our male and female aspects. Through the art of Middle

Eastern dance, we can begin to celebrate and value the power of the sacred feminine.

## The Triple Goddess: Maiden, Mother, Crone

Belly dancing is for *all* mobile women, the young, insecure woman, the pregnant woman, the mother, the woman going through a midlife crisis, as well as the grandmother. The maiden, mother, and crone are three faces of the Triple Goddess. They represent different stages of your life. Through ritual belly dance, the phases of your life may be celebrated and honored.

If you are a maiden, you signify the vitality of youth and are in the springtime of your life. You are usually between puberty and your twenties. In some Middle Eastern countries, it is customary for the hands and soles of a girl to be painted with henna, symbolizing the first menstrual blood and the young woman's ability to conceive and bear new life. As it has since the dawn of humanity, the belly dance can serve as your initiation dance into womanhood.

The mother represents nurturing and fertility. You may or may not work outside the home; you may or may not have children. If you are at this stage in life, you are the ferocious protector and caretaker of your own, whether they are your biological children or important people in your life. You may be married. This phase represents the summer of your life. You are typically between your mid twenties and thirties, although of course women are having children well into their forties and even fifties now! If you choose to become pregnant, the serpent-like movements of belly dance will prepare you for labor and delivery. Through belly dance, you honor the sacredness of motherhood.

The crone or wise woman is past menopause. As a natural spiritual leader and counselor, you have the wisdom of age and experience to draw from. As the powerful grandmother, in the winter of life, you represent the end of a cycle where death is a part of life. You are usually in your fifties and older. The wise woman symbolizes the heroic aspects of yourself, your inner strength, and your ability to overcome the trials and tribulations of life. Through belly dance, you may also honor the power and wisdom that later-life bring. You may honor the power of the Crone.

It appears to me there is often an unacknowledged stage in a woman's life between the time a woman's children reach puberty, and before she becomes the wise grandmother crone. You are in midlife. This is what I call the priestess aspect of the Goddess. Seasonally, this represents the autumn of your life. You may be in your thirties to forties.

As the priestess you turn inward, you may encounter the opportunity to engage in tremendous inner healing and may begin to connect to your spiritual power. A spiritual revival may occur, and you begin to train for the role of grandmother or spiritual leader. This period may be instigated by a new career, a divorce, and death of a parent, or any other so-called, *midlife crisis.* If you have the courage to face your pain and own your shadow, you may begin to understand what it is you didn't fulfill during your early years, what you missed out on, and what needs you may have failed to nurture or honor.

This is a time when spiritual growth can spiral, and you may transcend the self you have identified with all your life, finally connecting to a greater aspect of yourself. Through the belly dance, you can become a dancing priestess who honors the Divine Feminine within others and within yourself.

## Expressing the Energy of the Earth Goddess through Your Dance

In its purest and most natural state, the belly dance is a goddess dance. There is a spiritual being within you, and it is reflected in your movements. It is your responsibility to present the belly dance so as to express the magic, mystery, and power alive in yourself.

Through asking for divine guidance and through your intent and focus, you will create your very own sacred belly dance. This will uplift your spirit. In the process, you will raise the consciousness of humanity. You will become a living witness to the emergence of the light of the Divine Feminine after the long, dark night of patriarchy.

In this first dance ritual, I will show you how to express the powerful energy of the Earth Goddess through your belly dance. You will honor and celebrate the power and beauty of the feminine aspect of God, thus transforming your dance into a sacred dance. You can choose to practice this as a sacred rite for your own spiritual awakening and healing or for uplifting your audience as well. The beauty of this is your audience doesn't have to consciously know you are channeling divine energy; they will *feel* it from their heart and soul.

## Your Sacred Dance Ritual

You do not have to be an experienced dancer to express the Goddess in your dance. Your *intent and focus* is what lends power to your dance, not the steps. A lot of belly dance is interpretive and sheer improvisation. This is part of its appeal. It is best to record this sacred ritual prior to enacting it or have a friend read this to you as you enact your dance ritual.

The most important step to becoming a dance channel for the Goddess is your intent. Once you desire to receive and channel Her energy through your dance, and once you have convinced yourself you have the ability to connect to Her—and we all do—then it is simply a matter of focus.

1. Sit comfortably in a darkened room.
2. Take at least five slow, deep breaths, allowing all tension to drain from any part of your body or mind that needs relaxation.
3. Focus on your heart as you humbly imagine yourself standing in front of a beautiful and sacred temple.
4. After you step inside the temple, respectfully take your shoes off and look around you. You see the Goddess hovering in front of you in all Her feminine glory, bathed in a golden ball of cleansing light, Her arms joyously outstretched welcoming you home. Feel the warmth and healing energy of Her aura blending in with yours and know you are protected and nurtured by Her.
5. Let Her know you are open to Her divine guidance and light. Humbly ask Her to shine through in your dance for your highest good and the highest good of all who may bear witness to your dance.
6. Come out with a beautiful veil wrapped around you from the back and make a tent with your arms overhead. Do not reveal yourself yet, for the Goddess reveals Herself slowly and then only to those who seek Her with a pure heart.

7. As you begin your dance, focus on the light of the Goddess shining within your heart and flowing out through your eyes and out through the top of your head, spilling out over your body and or into your audience. Connect to the joy that is your dance and smile softly within. Take a few slow spins as you slowly unveil yourself.

8. Feel the energy of the Goddess as you look out from both your eyes and from between your eyes. Connect to yourself and or your audience through the use of your eyes. Feel the Goddess looking out onto Her creation through your eyes.

9. Allow your dance movements to spontaneously arise out of your heart and soul. Do not worry so much what your movements look like, but more what they *feel* like. The power of your dance is not in your dance ability or technique, but in sharing your strong connection to the Great Mother. Stay connected to Her presence and then express Her transforming, healing energy outward.

10. As you continue your dance in this heightened state of awareness, you will feel refreshed, nourished, and joyful by the end of your dance. If you have an audience, they will feel it too.


It is best to practice this ritual in the privacy of your own home to connect you to the presence of the Divine Feminine in your day-to-day life as well as in your dance. I have used this little meditation both to start off my day and prior to performances. For the latter, finding a space may take some ingenuity. However, while in a restaurant, I have used a tiny closet, a restroom stall, or simply sat in my car prior to a show. I have been amazed at the added energy and joy that this powerful visualization brings to my dance.

Often the audience is so mesmerized, they forget to tip me! However, I usually get hired by one of the restaurant patrons for a special occasion event instead. At a dance show in Reno, Nevada, a contest judge once said to me, "When you dance, you look as though you are in bliss." I am!

## Enacting Your Very Own Rite of Passage Ceremonies

Today in our post-industrial world, we lack rite of passage ceremonies to mark the different stages of our lives. In early times, through powerful rites of passage, both sexes entered the different phases of life in a powerful and meaningful manner. With the belly dance, you too can honor and celebrate the different phases of your life and celebrate the power and beauty of the feminine aspect of the Creator. Soon, you will find yourself in a beautiful and sacred temple where as a tribal woman you will enact and celebrate your present stage of your life through belly dance.

No matter what phase of life you are in, you will use the magic and power of ritual to celebrate these important aspects of your life. You may enact all the phases you have already lived or simply the one you are currently in. It is up to you. In our culture, we already have ceremonies for weddings and birthdays, so I will not include these. You can always make up your own based on what you learn below. The following ceremonies are simply guidelines for you to follow or from which to make up your own rituals.

It is more powerful to enact these rites with a group of women (priestesses) you respect and trust. You may choose to enact just one or all of the rites below. If you never had the opportunity to celebrate your first period or to honor your pregnant self, it is never too late to do so. Below are some suggestions.

Imagine a beautiful and sacred temple where tribal women and priestesses gather together to enact and celebrate the various stages of their lives: the advent of menstruation and womanhood, the miracle of pregnancy and motherhood, the growing pains and sufferings of midlife, and the wisdom that old age bring. You will reconnect to your ancient roots, to a time when humanity honored the feminine mysteries and spirituality.

Call the priestesses to your temple. Begin each ceremony by invoking the Earth Goddess through a sacred candle dance. With lighted candles, you and the priestesses dance slow undulating circular movements and figure-eights to music that you find soothing and healing until you feel the Goddess descend upon you.

### Sacred Moon Dance

Belly dance may serve as an initiation dance into womanhood. Through this dance, you honor the *virgin/maiden* aspect of the Goddess. Your first ceremony involves reclaiming the sacred rite of menstruation. This is best enacted while menstruating, but not necessary. As stated previously in this chapter, in some Middle Eastern countries, it is customary for the hands and soles of a girl to be painted with henna to symbolize the first menstrual blood and the young woman's ability to conceive and bear new life.

1. The priestesses dress you in a comfortable, flowing white robe made of light material, such as polyester, chiffon, or cotton.
2. They then paint your face with white moons against a red background, symbolizing your cycles' natural connection to the moon (an old Native American custom). They also paint your soles and hands with henna (an ancient Middle Eastern custom).

141

3. They explain to you that when women used to live in nature, their periods coincided with the cycles of the moon. What's more, women instinctively understood the hormonal shifts that occur during menstruation move them into a place where change or new ways of being more easily occur.[55]

4. The priestesses explain to you how your cycle of hormonal change prepares you for the process of creating a space in your life for new things each month; you understand this is a very powerful time for creativity, transformation, and healing.[56]

5. With candles still lit, the high priestess gives you a basket filled with beautiful red rose petals. Roses have long been used as symbols of the feminine.

6. Play slow, mysterious music. For example, the famous song "Blue Moon" would set a nice tone for this ceremony.

7. You are then lovingly encircled by the priestesses as you offer up the rose petals to the moon in a beautiful moon dance, comprised of flowing, watery movements of the hands, arms, torso, and legs. The watery movements are symbolic of your sacred blood that nourishes the earth every month.

8. Toward the end of your dance, the priestesses ask you to focus on one thing you would like to change in your life. Focus on this as you take the petals with your hands and toss them up to the moon. Or hold the basket overhead, spin quickly and allow the petals to fall naturally to the earth.

9. Finally, choose a spiritual name symbolic of your transformation into womanhood (also an old Native American tradition).

## *Dance of the Serpent - Celebrating Fertility and Pregnancy*

Throughout pregnancy, the serpent-like movements of belly dance prepare a woman for childbirth. Belly dance is an ancient fertility dance. Through this dance we honor the sacredness of pregnancy and motherhood.

Don't panic, you don't have to go out and buy a snake for this ceremony; a fake wooden or rubber snake will do. You may also use an imaginary snake. It is time we learn to get over the fears we may have of snakes. Remember, at one time, your ancestor's *revered* snakes as symbols of wisdom, rebirth, and regeneration! In the temple of Dendera, Egypt, snakes were protectors of the home. Today, the medical profession still uses the symbol of two intertwined snakes to symbolize the healing profession. This is a remnant of ancient times, before the snake received a "bad rap" from religion.

1. The priestesses bring a basket to you. The basket is covered and carrying a sleeping snake. The snake is powerful but harmless. The high priestess instructs you to dance in the middle of an enclosed circle. The other women place rocks on the ground to trace a sacred circle around you. These rocks symbolize the power and strength you possess during pregnancy as you create a life, and during motherhood, as you nurture, support, and protect a brand new life from infancy unto adulthood. It takes a powerful human being to accomplish this!

2. Begin a slow, sensuous dance to slow, sensuous music. When the moment feels right, slowly take your power animal out of its basket and dance with it. As you roll your belly and dance with snake arms

143

become one with its mysterious powers of regeneration and rebirth. Release any fears and take on the powers of the snake! In ancient times, snakes and women were connected.

3.  At the end of your dance, wrap your snake around your hips, close to your lower back. This is where ancient Indian texts state a sleeping serpent lies, coiled but ready to rise up from your spine and transform you.

4.  Slowly uncoil the snake and raise it overhead symbolizing the energy of the Kundalini rising up your spine and bringing forth creative and healing powers to both you and your children.

5.  The priestesses bow before you, honoring your sacred and magical power to create and support a new life.

### *Initiation into the Underworld*

It is on the floor that a woman's bond to the earth is expressed most strongly. The floor dance represents a descent into the Underworld where a woman in midlife owns her pain and embraces her shadow. She then transforms old ways of being and emerges victoriously as the priestess, possessed of her feminine power and authority. The sword symbolizes the heroic aspects of a woman, her inner strength, her ability to overcome the trials and tribulations of life. Through this dance, we honor the power and wisdom that midlife brings.

1.  The high priestess tells you that soon you will become a priestess yourself! She hands you the sacred sword of wisdom. She explains this sword has been handed down from the sacred lineage of Isis, the

ancient Egyptian Mother Goddess of the Universe. This then is an ancient sacred sword thousands of years old. Anyone who dances with this sword will energetically receive its wisdom.

2. The high priestess instructs you to begin your dance on the floor in order to honor your bond to the earth and to symbolize your descent into the Underworld.

3. In this dance within the protective circle of the priestesses, connect to your pain, your grief, your anger, or any other aspect of yourself that cries out for healing.

4. The high priestess plays fiery, emotional, and passionate music to help you express any feelings that may lie buried. Dance these out!

5. On the floor, roll your head and hair. Slowly stand up and with figure-eight hips and shimmies dance yourself into frenzy, releasing the pain of a lifetime.

6. Finally, pick up your sword and pierce the air filled with your pain. This piercing represents confronting your pain and your inner demons. With this very ancient and powerful sword of wisdom, symbolically trace your circle of power on the floor in front of you and take a giant step into your power. Touch the earth with your sword and then raise your sword up toward the heavens to reflect the unity of Earth and Heaven, of the feminine and the masculine. You have now been initiated into a beautiful and wise priestess.

### *Dance of the Earth Goddess*

Now, you have reached the winter of your life and are in your full power. You have become the high priestess well qualified to lead others' ceremonies and your own ceremony. Having become the epitome of the wise old woman through your dance you spontaneously channel the healing energy of the Earth Goddess who resides within all women. Whenever anyone needs your wisdom or counsel you joyfully dance for them; you heal them by channeling the splendor of the Earth Goddess out through your body unto their energy field. Although your words are powerful and bring much insight, it is through your dance that someone in need of healing energetically receives your wisdom. Your dance revives and heals others on many levels.

1. You are dressed in a splendid, fiery, orange-red robe with a purple scarf wrapped around your hips and a purple veil wrapped around your neck from behind trailing down the front. Red symbolizes your ability to connect to the earth and the power of your passion. Purple symbolizes the power of your spirit.

2. You dance to fiery drum music using sharp, strong hip drops, hip lifts, shimmies, and pelvic drops and lifts. You dance without a sword or basket for you no longer need symbolic props to remind you of the power of the great Mother Goddess. You have become Her living embodiment and joyfully share Her knowledge with all who seek your wisdom. As a natural spiritual leader and wise woman, you possess the wisdom of age and experience. As you dance your dance of power, the younger priestesses gather around you to honor the crone aspect of the Goddess.

**Raising the Consciousness of Our Planet**

Congratulations! You have now begun to transform your old ways of being through honoring your heretofore-ignored life passages. You have begun to flood the darkness in your life with divine light. If all of us honored our lives in this manner, the consciousness of our planet would transform overnight! I salute the power of the Divine Feminine within you!

**The Goddess Dancing**

"Through these experiences and my association with other belly dancers, my vision has been nurtured and given life. Intuition and clairvoyant perception tells me that all of us who are drawn to this expressive art have some role to play in rekindling ancient spiritual truth, in restoring wholeness to ourselves, and in helping humanity prepare for an evolutionary shift into a new, more harmonious way of life. The power that we now hold as a community is in our growing numbers, in our nurturing of ourselves, giving support to one another, and holding fast to our visions of a more peaceful, loving world."[57]

# Appendix—Resources

## Music Sites for Belly Dance

### CD Baby
CDbaby.com

I recommend Tim Rayborn, under world music


### The International Academy of Middle Eastern Dance (IAMED)
Music, instructional videos and video footage

www.bellydance.org


### Maqam Music
Fine Arabic and Middle Eastern Music

http://www.maqam.com/


### Music of Lebanon
http://www.musicoflebanon.com/

Listen to sample CD tracks


### Pe-Ko International
A leading world music source

http://www.pekorecords.com/

**Rashid Music Sales**

Established in 1934. They claim to be the largest and oldest distributor
of Arabic Music
http://www.rashid.com/
Music Excerpts available

**Shimmy Shimmy**

Shimmyshimmy.com
Music Excerpts available.

## Recommended CD's

I own all of the selections below and heartily recommend them:

**A Celebration of World Dance, Sarasvati**, by Desert Wind – Moving tribal rhythms

**Alabina,** by Alabina - A wonderful combination of Spanish & Arabic music

**Belly Dance Fever** – A compilation of songs from various artists

**Bellydance from Egypt "Gamil Gamal",** by Bashir Abdel' Aal

**Belly Dance Superstars, Volume 1 and 2** – Fabulous rhythms and energy

**Belly Dance with Samara** by Setrak

**Best of Arabian Bellydance** by Emad Sayyah, Aboud Abdel Al and others

**Best of Baladi and Saidi** by Hossam Ramzy

**Best of Amr Diab** – Arabic pop music

**Eternal Egypt** by Phil Thornton & Hossam Ramzy – Ancient, mystical sounds

**Zakharafa** by Helm - Classical Egyptian & original compositions, Upper Egypt style.

**Luxor to Isna** by Musicians of the Nile

**Mezdeke 4 and Mezdeke 6** by Misir Danslari – Arabic pop music

**Middle Eastern Odyssey** by Adam Basma

**Migration** by Gypsy Caravan and Friends – Tribal music

**Moon Over Cairo Amayaguena** by Amaya – One of my favorite CD's!

## Belly Dance Merchandise

You will find everything you need for belly dance on these sites including costumes, music, DVDs, hip scarves, unitards and veils.

## BellyDance Shoppe

http://www.bellydanceshoppe.com/

## Scheherazade Imports

www.scheherezadeimports.com

## Shimmy Shimmy

Belly dance costumes, hip scarves, clothing, jewelry, accessories, music & props

www.shimmyshimmy.com

## Jodette International

Belly dance books, videos, DVD's, and cassette tapes. Jodette also sells costumes.

http://www.jodette.com/ 1-916-448-1665

## Silk Veils

Divine dancing veils and silk clothing. Absolutely gorgeous! www.akaisilks.com

## Gina, The Little Gypsy

Complete Costumes available from $100.00 to $1,000.00. Hip scarves &

veils available from $35.00-$85.00. Sizes available from petite to voluptuous. http://www.littlegypsy.net 1-916-531-2541.

**Lila's Belly Dancing Bazaar**

Offering authentic belly dance costumes completely handmade in the Middle East for the belly dance professional, as well as for the amateur belly dancer. www.bellydancecostumes.com

**Fatima's Bazaar and Cultural Dance Studio**

Fatima is one of the Middle Eastern Dance world's most prominent vendors. http://www.fatimasbazaar.com 1-916-482-3568

**Turkish Emporium**

Beautiful costumes, Turkish style
www.turkish-emporium.com

Daleela Morad

# Belly Dance Festivals

### Rakkassah Festival

Rakkasah West is the largest Middle Eastern Folk Festival and Fantasy Bazaar in the world. The Festival takes place once a year in March in California.  The festivities are kicked off with a weeklong workshop featuring internationally known belly dancing, folk dancing, and music teachers.
The festival itself is open to the general public and is suitable for people of all ages. You will find exotic costuming, hip scarves, musical instruments, jewelry, and decor for your home, henna painting, dancers, dancers, dancers and more dancers. There is also an annual Rakkassah East Festival held in October in Somerset New Jersey.
Rakkasah West and East:  http://www.rakkasah.com/

### Desert Dance Festival

Usually occurs every autumn in San Jose, California. The 2-day dance festival is open to the public and highlights the Middle Eastern Dance Community with dance workshops, fashion shows, vendors selling exotic costumes, musical instruments, jewelry, henna painting, and of course beautiful performing dancers. Contact Dunia for more information at: duniadancer@yahoo.com. http://www.desertdance.com/

## Belly Dance Magazines

### Belly Dance, a Raqs Sharqi Magazine

Explores the many facets of traditional and modern belly dance and Middle Eastern-influenced music that reaches out to talented dancers and musicians throughout the US. **http://www.bellydancemag.com/**

### The Gilded Serpent

An online magazine with fascinating articles about belly dancing past and present. http://www.gildedserpent.com

### Zaghareet

A belly dance magazine with articles on travel, musicians, dancers, troupes, and more...
http://www.zaghareet.freeservers.com/magazine.html

### Jareeda

An international news magazine for Middle Eastern dance
http://www.jareeda.com/

## Recommended Videos/DVD's

**Afrika Mother of Dance Part 2: Primordial Rhythms.** Journey to Africa with Mesmera.

**Bellydance Fitness for Beginners** by Veena and Neena

**Belly Dance Live, Part 2, Classical Belly Dance,** by Keti Sharif, for intermediate level dancers.

**Dances from Egypt** by Aisha Ali. One of my favorite documentary videos!

**Dance of the Serpent** with Mesmera. Includes both instruction and performance. Mesmera will mesmerize you with her Boa constrictor.

**Desert Wanderers** by Hahbi 'Ru. It's like going back in time to an ancient past.

**Emerald Dreams** by Tamalyn Dallal. A beautiful belly dance concert! I highly recommend this performance video.

**Gypsy Fire** by Amaya. Passionate Spanish Arabic dances and dance Instruction.

**Hip Hop Hip Drop** by Rania. A great *workout* video.

**Lifting the Veil of Time** by Artemis Mourat. An informative and entertaining *history* of belly dance.

**Mezdulene's Veiled Visions** Intermediate veil instruction and performance by Mezdulene.

**Secrets of the Centre** by Keti Sharif. Instruction for beginners.

**Suhaila Unveiled** by Suhaila Salimpour. A powerful belly dance performance.

**The Art of Oriental Dance** by Majida Magdalena A beautiful performance video.

**The Sensual Art of Belly Dance – Beyond Basic Dance**
Intermediate instruction by Veena & Neena Bidasha.

# Endnotes

[1] Kundalini Yoga,
http://www.sanatansociety.org/chakras/kundalini_yoga.htm

[2] Delilah, "Reviving Ophelia Through Belly Dance: Does Belly Dance Offer Women a More Positive Self-Image?" *Visionary Dance Productions*, (The Image We Are Sold), http://www.visionarydance.com/revivingophelia.html

[3] Ibid.

[4] Delilah, "Reviving Ophelia Through Belly Dance: Does Belly Dance Offer Women a More Positive Self-Image?" *Visionary Dance Productions*, (Preface), http://www.visionarydance.com/revivingophelia.html.

[5] Melanie Pitre, "Plastic Surgery Addicts" November 5, 2007, *American Chronicle,*
http://www.americanchronicle.com/articles/viewArticle.asp?articleID=42254

[6] Atea, "Creating Inner Peace with Oriental Dance," *Magical Motion*,
http://www.magicalmotion.com/bellydance1.html

[7] Ibid.

[8] Ibid.

[9] Journal of American College Health, "1995 National College Health Risk Behavior Survey," *Journal of American College Health,* (September 1997), www.sa.rochester.edu/masa/stats.php.

[10] Hanson, R.F., and others, "Factors Relating to the Reporting of Childhood Sexual Assault," *Child Abuse and Neglect* 23 (1999): 559-569.

[11] Lipschitz, "Belly Dance and Healing from Sexual Trauma," *Gilded Serpent Magazine,*
http://www.gildedserpent.com/articles23/lucyraperecoverywdance.htm

[12] Gioseffi, *Earth Dancing*, 192.

[13] Lafata, "Embodied Sexuality & Female Power," *Bellydance As Healing Dance*, March 2002, http://www.visionarydance.com/HealingDanceArc.html

[14] Arav, *Grandmother's Secrets: The Ancient Rituals and Healing Power of Belly Dancing,* 59.

[15] Gioseffi, *Earth Dancing*, 43.

[16] Stahlman, "The Spirit of the Ouled Nayl: A Workshop with Amel Tafsout," *Tribal Talk: The Voice of FatChanceBellyDance*, Spring 1997.

[17] Stunning Tents Company, "The Ouled Nayl: A Brief Portrait," *The Stunning Tents Company*, http://www.stunningtents.co.uk/Ouled_nail_culture.html.

[18] Gioseffi, *Earth Dancing*, 38.

[19] Sinclair Intimacy Institute, *The Better Sex: Making Sex Fun (with games & toys)*, DVD, Learning Corp Revision, 2002.

[20] Ibid.

[21] Friedman, *Romance is a Decision*, cassette.

[22] Ibid.

[23] See note 32.

[24] Anand, *The Art of Sexual Ecstasy: The Path of Sacred Sexuality for Western Lovers*, 33-38.

[25] Ibid., 59-68.

[26] Ibid., 71-78.

[27] Ibid., 96-105.

[28] Ibid., 10-12.

[29] Keesling, *Making Love Series, Vol 11: Tantric Lovemaking,* VHS.

[30] Ibid.

[31] Ibid.

[32] Ibid.

[33] Gioseffi, *Earth Dancing*, 28.

[34] Rose, *The Path of the Priestess: A Guidebook for Awakening the Divine Feminine*, p. 140.

[35] Buonaventura, *Serpent of the Nile*, 30-32.

[36] Gioseffi, *Earth Dancing*, 39.

[37] Stewart, *Sacred Woman, Sacred Dance*, 70.

[38] Ibid., 37.

[39] Duricy, "Black Madonnas," *The Marian Library/International Marian Research Institute,* March 23, 2005, http://www.udayton.edu/mary/meditations/blackmdn.html.

[40] Estes, *Women Who Run with the Wolves: Myths and Stories of the Wild Woman Archetype*, 4.

[41] Budapest, *The Holy Book of Women's Mysteries*, p. 12

[42] See note 7.

[43] Buonaventura, *Serpent of the Nile*, 34-35.

[44] Ibid.

[45] Stewart, *Sacred Woman, Sacred Dance*, 38-41.

[46] Ibid., 40.

[47] Ibid.

[48] Ibid.

[49] *Wikepedia, The Free Encyclopedia Online,* s.v. "Eleusinian Mysteries," http://en.wikipedia.org/wiki/Eleusinian_Mysteries.

[50] *Wikepedia, The Free Encyclopedia Online,* s.v. "Mystery Schools," http://en.wikipedia.org/wiki/Mystery_schools.

[51] Pettigrew, *The Burning Times*, VHS, directed by Donna Read.

[52] Ibid.

[53] Ibid.

[54] Rose, *The Path of the Priestess: A Guidebook for Awakening the Divine Feminine*, 157.

[55] Wind, *New Moon Rising—Reclaiming the Sacred Rites of Menstruation*, 34.

[56] Ibid.

[57] Sophia, "The Goddess is Dancing," *Magical Motion*, http://www.bellydancingvideo.com/bellydance1.html

# Bibliography

Anand, Margo. *The Art of Sexual Ecstasy: The Path of Sacred Sexuality for Western Lovers.* Los Angeles: Jeremy P. Tarcher, Inc., 1989.

Rosina-Fawzia Al-Rawi. *Grandmother's Secrets: The Ancient Rituals and Healing Power of Belly Dancing.* New York: Interlink Books, 1999.

Atea. "Creating Inner Peace with Oriental Dance." *Magical Motion.* http://www.magicalmotion.com/bellydance1.html.

Brown University Health Education, "Eating Concerns and Men," Adapted from the *Boston College Eating Awareness Team*, written by Boston College Counseling Services http://www.brown.edu/Student_Services/Health_Services/Health_Education/nutrition/ec_men.htm.

Buonaventura, Wendy. *Serpent of the Nile: Women and Dance in the Arab World.* New York: Interlink Books, 1998.

Delilah. "Reviving Ophelia Through Belly Dance: Does Belly Dance Offer Women a More Positive Self-Image?". *Visionary Dance Productions.* http://www.visionarydance.com/revivingophelia.html.

Estes, Clarissa Pinkola, Ph.D. *Women Who Run with the Wolves: Myths and Stories of the Wild Woman Archetype.* New York: Ballantine Books, 1992.

Friedman, Dr. Ellen. *Romance is a Decision.* Cassette.

Gioseffi, Daniela. *Earth Dancing: Mother Nature's Oldest Rite.* Harrisburg: Stackpole Books, 1980.

Gurmukh. *Kundalini Yoga.* VHS. CMM Living Arts. 2000.

Hanson, R.F., Resnick, H.S., Saunders, B.E., Kilpatrick, D.G., Best, C. "Factors Relating to the Reporting of Childhood Sexual Assault," *Child Abuse and Neglect* 23 (1999): 559-569.

Daleela Morad

Hilber, Alison and Joslyn Jordan. "Love Me… Love My Belly!" *Planet Vermont Quarterly*. http://planetvermont.com/pvq/v9n2/belly.html.

Journal of American College Health. "1995 National College Health Risk Behavior Survey," *Journal of American College Health,* (September 1997), www.sa.rochester.edu/masa/stats.php.

Keesling, Barbara, Ph.D. *Playboy's Making Love Series, Vol. II: Tantric Lovemaking*. VHS. Playboy Entertainment Group Inc., 1995.

Lafata, Lorraine, MSW, LICSW. "Embodied Sexuality & Female Power." *Bellydance As Healing Dance*. March 2002. http://www.visionarydance.com/HealingDanceArc.html.

Latif, Angie. *Arabia Online*. www.arabia.com (accessed January 2003; article title not found).

Lipschitz, Lucy. "Belly Dance and Healing from Sexual Trauma." *Gilded Serpent Magazine.* http://www.gildedserpent.com/articles23/lucyraperecoverywdance.htm.

Rose, Sharron. *The Path of the Priestess: A Guidebook for Awakening the Divine Feminine*. Rochestor: Inner Traditions International, 2003.

Sinclair Intimacy Institute. *The Better Sex: Making Sex Fun (with games & toys)*. VHS. Learning Corp Revision, 2002.

Sophia, Christina. "The Goddess is Dancing." *Magical Motion*. Fall 1999. http://www.magicalmotion.com/bellydance1.html.

Stahlman, Kathy. "The Spirit of the Ouled Nayl: A Workshop with Amel Tafsout." *Tribal Talk: The Voice of FatChanceBellyDance*. Spring 1997.

Stewart, Iris. *Sacred Woman, Sacred Dance*. Rochester: Inner Traditions International, 2000.

Stunning Tents Company. "The Ouled Nayl: A Brief Portrait." *The Stunning Tents Company.*
http://www.stunningtents.co.uk/Ouled_nail_culture.html.

Tyldesley, Joyce. *Daughters of Isis: Women of Ancient Egypt.* New York: Penguin Books, 1994.

Wind, Linda Heron, Ph.D. *New Moon Rising: Reclaiming the Sacred Rites of Menstruation.* Chicago: Delphi Press Inc., 1995.

Witcombe, Christopher L.C.E. "Earth Mother—Mother Goddess," *Women in Prehistory: The Venus of Willendorf,*
http://witcombe.sbc.edu/willendorf/willendorfgoddess.html, 2003.

Woolger, Jennifer and Roger. *The Goddess Within.* New York: Ballantine Books, 1989.

Kundalini Yoga, http://www.sanatansociety.org/chakras/kundalini_yoga.htm

LaVergne, TN USA
08 September 2009
157119LV00003B/27/P